recipes

for y

grilling

machine

recipes
for your
grilling
machine

carolyn humphries

foulsham
LONDON • NEW YORK • TORONTO • SYDNEY

foulsham

The Publishing House, Bennetts Close, Cippenham, Slough,
Berkshire, SL1 5AP, England

ISBN 0-572-03118-1

Cover photograph © Phil Wilkins

A CIP record for this book is available from the British Library

With thanks to Breville and Morphy Richards for the loan of grills used in the
testing of these recipes

Printed and bound in Great Britain by Mackays of Chatham plc, Chatham, Kent

CONTENTS

INTRODUCTION

We've always known that grilling or broiling food is preferable to frying – it is a much healthier option because you don't have to cook in loads of added fat. Grilling also helps meat retain more B vitamins than frying.

The advantages of an electric health grill over a conventional grill are that it is quick and convenient, and often uses less fuel. It also allows the fat in the food and any juices to drip off into a handy container; the fat can then be spooned off and the juices used for an accompanying sauce, when appropriate. Food cooked on the grill has that attractive 'griddled' look as well.

You may have thought you can only cook burgers and steaks on your grilling machine, but you'd be wrong. You can cook everything from kebabs to fish, vegetables to fruits and, of course, the most sensational toasted sandwiches and other snacks. This book shows you exactly how to do all these things, and every delicious, innovative recipe will help you make the most of your new gadget, so you can enjoy delicious, healthy meals every day.

USING YOUR HEALTH GRILL

I n this chapter, you'll find everything you need to know to get the
best out of your appliance.

Before you use your grill for the first time
- Remove all packaging.
- Wipe over the plates and then the outside with a clean, damp cloth.
- Wash the drip tray in warm, soapy water, then rinse, dry and put in place.
- Place the grill on a flat, heat-resistant surface (I always put mine on a large, heat-resistant chopping board).
- Make sure the cord does not hang over the edge of the work surface.
- Make sure the cord is completely unravelled.

WARNING

**Do not put the cord, plug or body of the grill in water
or any other liquid.**

When you are ready to use the grill
- Make sure the drip tray is in the correct position. Never use without the drip tray in place.
- Close the machine for efficient heating up.
- Insert the plug into a suitable socket and switch on. The red 'power on' light should glow.
- Turn the heat control up as high as possible to heat quickly. The grill is ready to cook when the indicator light glows (see your manufacturer's instruction booklet). If not cooking on the hottest setting, turn the grill down to the temperature you require.
- When using the cooker for the first time, a fine smoke haze may appear as the components heat up. This is normal.
- Oil the plates, if appropriate (see individual recipes).

Basic instructions for grilling

The grill can be used open or closed. All the recipes in this book give you instructions for the different methods, as appropriate.

In the closed position, your grill will cook food in half the time it takes to cook both sides separately. Cooking with the lid closed is suitable for firm foods, such as steaks, sausages, bacon, vegetables and toasted sandwiches. The open position is more suitable for soft foods that would squash completely flat with the weight of the lid.

Some machines have a variable top plate, which enables you to cook more foods with the lid down – such as thicker meats, softer fish, seafood and fruits. You can also toast buns for burgers. If your grill has fixed plates, you can obtain a similar effect for some foods by supporting the lid clip on a cork or similar heat-resistant object, so it holds the lid in an open position, just resting on the food. Do not use anything to support the clip that is flammable, metallic or liable to melt. You may need to rearrange the food during cooking, as this method won't grill as evenly as variable plates.

WARNING
The machine plates and body will get really hot during cooking so avoid touching any part except the handle.

- Oil the food, or drain off any marinade, if necessary.
- Lay the food on the preheated grill plates. Close the lid, if appropriate. If the lid is to remain open, the food must be pressed gently with a spatula to obtain the griddle marks on the surface.
- Cook for the stated time, turning if recommended during cooking.
- If food is very fatty, drain the drip tray during cooking, to prevent fat overflowing, and replace immediately.
- When the food is cooked, open the lid, if necessary, and remove the food using a non-metallic spatula or tongs.
- Reheat the grill before cooking a second batch of food.

WARNING
Do not use metal utensils as they could damage the plates.

Basic instructions for toasting

- Close the machine and plug in as before.
- Turn the setting to 'low' or 'sandwich', if your machine has a variable setting.
- Butter or oil the filled bread or rolls on the outside.
- Place on the hot plate, lower and fasten the lid. Cook for the recommended time.
- Lift the lid and remove the toasted food with non-metallic tongs.
- For thicker snacks, either use an adjustable grill or support the lid on a cork or similar heat-resistant object (see page 10).

Cleaning your grill

- Always unplug the grill after use.
- Remove and empty the drip tray. Wash in warm, soapy water. Dry with a soft cloth.
- If your grill has fixed plates, wipe these immediately, while still hot, with a clean, soft cloth or kitchen paper (paper towels).
- If there are baked-on food particles, mix some warm water with detergent and squeeze over the residue, then clean off with a non-abrasive plastic scourer or brush.
- If the grill has removable plates, leave the machine to cool down, then remove them and wash them in warm, soapy water or put in the dishwasher.
- Wipe over all the rest of the machine with a clean, damp cloth or kitchen paper.
- Always replace the drip tray and put away the cord in the cord storage.

WARNING

Never immerse the machine in water.

Safety tips

- Do not put the cord, plug or body of the grill in water or any other liquid.
- Always make sure there is adequate air space around the appliance when in use.
- Make sure it is on a heat-resistant, level, dry surface.
- Avoid contact with any flammable materials while in use – such as curtains, cloths, kitchen paper (paper towels), wall coverings, etc.
- Do not use the appliance outdoors.

- Do not place it against any other appliance when in use.
- Do not line the plates with foil or other materials.
- The machine plates and body will get very hot during cooking, so avoid touching any part except the handle.
- Keep children away from the appliance when in use as it becomes very hot.
- Do not leave the appliance unattended when in use.

Cooking tips

- For best results, always cook foods of similar thickness at the same time.
- Check food during cooking. If some pieces are not browning on top because they are thinner than other pieces, turn them over. In the same way, round foods, such as sausages, benefit from being turned gradually during cooking to get an even griddled effect.
- If you have marinated food before grilling, drain it well and pat dry, if necessary, before placing on the grill plates or it will generate too much steam and the results may be disappointingly soggy. Also, if the marinade has a high sugar content, this could cause the surface of the food to burn or the plates to scorch, so take care, check often and don't overcook.
- For best results, thaw frozen foods before grilling. Fish, in particular, produces too much liquid when cooked from frozen.
- Do not sprinkle salt on food before cooking: it will toughen the surface. A little salt in a marinade is okay, however.
- Do not keep pricking meat or poultry during cooking or all the juices will run out, making it dry and tough.
- Thin foods, like vegetables and fruit, will grill more evenly if brushed with oil or marinade before cooking, rather than just oiling the plates. However, thick meats, fish and poultry are best grilled on oiled plates.
- Avoid cooking chops with bones that protrude above the meat: these may stop the meat from coming into contact with the hot plates and the results could be disappointing. If your meat does have protruding bones, remove them before grilling.
- To prevent sausages bursting during cooking, parboil them first. Parboiling will also tenderise fatty ribs before grilling.

HEALTHY EATING

I t is important for all of us that we eat well and wisely. Here are a few tips to a good, balanced diet – with a little help from your health grill, of course!

- Eat at least five portions of fruit and vegetables a day (a glass of pure juice – fresh, canned or long-life – can count as one). These help maintain your body and mind, supplying vital vitamins and minerals. You can use your grill to cook lots of vegetables and fruits with the minimum of added fat but remember, raw ones are good for you too!
- Eat plenty of starchy carbohydrates for energy and warmth. At least half of your food every day should come from bread, cereals, potatoes, pasta, rice and so on, especially wholemeal and unrefined products. Your grill is great for toasting bread, crumpets, bagels, etc., as well as making toasted sandwiches and panini. Use it for almost-fat-free potato snacks too – see my recipe on page 114.
- Eat two or three portions of protein each day. This is found in meat, poultry, fish, eggs and dairy products like cheese, milk and yoghurt. There is also vegetable protein in pulses – such as dried peas, lentils and beans (including baked beans) – as well as tofu, Quorn and soya products. Your grill will cook most of these to perfection.
- Eat lots of fibre to keep your digestive system moving. You can get this from your fruit and vegetables, especially if you eat any of their skins that are edible, such as on apples and potatoes (see my recipe on page 115). Dried fruits, breakfast cereals and bread (especially the wholegrain varieties), seeds and nuts also contain high levels of fibre.
- Your body needs fat for warmth and to keep your organs functioning properly. However, it only needs a very little, and all the fat you require is contained naturally in foods, especially dairy products, meat, poultry, fish, nuts, seeds and cereals. So don't slap butter on bread with a trowel (add just a scraping for toasted sandwiches). Use just a little olive or sunflower oil when greasing your grill and just watch the excess fat drip away from meat, fish, poultry – and even cheese!
- Avoid extra sugar and too many sugary or fatty foods.

BASIC FOOD HYGIENE

A hygienic cook is a healthy cook – so please bear the following in mind when you're preparing food.

- Always wash your hands before preparing food.
- Always wash and dry fresh produce before use.
- Don't lick your fingers.
- Don't keep tasting and stirring with the same spoon. Use a clean spoon every time you taste the food when you're making fresh salsas, etc., to go with your grills.
- Don't put raw and cooked meat on the same shelf in the fridge. Store raw meat on the bottom shelf, so it can't drip over other foods. Keep all perishable foods wrapped separately. Don't overfill the fridge or it will remain too warm.
- Never use a cloth to wipe down a chopping board that you have been using for cutting up meat, for instance, then use the same cloth to wipe down your work surfaces or the health grill – you will simply spread germs. Always wash your cloth well in hot, soapy water and, ideally, use an anti-bacterial kitchen cleaner on all surfaces too.
- Always transfer leftovers to a clean container and cover with a lid, clingfilm (plastic wrap) or foil. Cool as quickly as possible, then store in the fridge. Never put any warm food in the fridge.

NOTES ON THE RECIPES

- I used a Breville HG17 and a Morphy Richards 44710 Health Grill to test the recipes. If your model is smaller, you may need to cook some foods in batches. If so, keep each batch warm in a low oven while you cook the remainder. Cover the food if it needs to remain moist, but leave uncovered if you want the outside fairly dry – such as on potatoes or sandwiches. Always reheat the grill between batches.
- All ingredients are given in metric, imperial and American measures. Follow one set only in a recipe. American terms are given in brackets.
- The ingredients are listed in the order in which they are used in the recipe.
- All spoon measures are level: 1 tsp=5 ml; 1 tbsp=15 ml.
- Eggs are medium unless otherwise stated.
- Always wash, peel, core and seed, if necessary, fresh produce before use.
- Seasoning and the use of strongly flavoured ingredients such as garlic or chillies are very much a matter of personal taste, so adjust them to suit your own palate.
- Fresh herbs are great for garnishing and adding flavour. Pots of them are available in all good supermarkets. Keep your favourite ones on the windowsill and water regularly. Jars of ready-prepared herbs, like coriander (cilantro) and lemon grass, and frozen ones – chopped parsley in particular – are also very useful. I use a mixture of these and dried ones in the recipes. I don't recommend that you substitute dried for fresh when only fresh is called for – there is always a good reason why!
- All can and packet sizes are approximate as they vary from brand to brand. For example, if I call for a 400 g/14 oz/large can of tomatoes and yours is a 397 g can – that's fine.
- Cooking times are approximate and should be used as a guide only. Always check food is piping hot and cooked through before serving.

COOKING TIMES

These cooking times will provide you with a useful guide but you need to remember that they are intended as a guide only, as all grills vary. Always cook for the shorter time, then check, then cook for a little longer if necessary – that way you won't end up with burnt rations. If cooking with the lid up, the cooking time given is per side.

Food		Grilling time for closed grill or per side (in minutes)
Beef	Fillet, 2.5 cm/1 in thick	3–8 (from rare to well done)
	Rump/sirloin, 1 cm/½ in thick	2–6 (from rare to well done)
	Thin (minute) steak	1–2
Lamb	Chops/cutlets/steaks, thick	3–6 (from pink to well done)
	Chops/cutlets/steaks, thin	2–4 (from pink to well done)
Pork	Chops/steaks	6–8
	Escalopes	2–3
Gammon	Steaks	3–6
	Bacon rashers	1–2
Chicken	Breasts, boneless	6–8
	Thighs, boneless	5–6
	Legs/thighs, with bone	10–13
	Portions/spatchcocked poussins	13–15
	Wings	8–10
Duck	Breasts, boneless	4–7 (from pink to well-done)
	Portions	10–15

Food		Grilling time for closed grill or per side (in minutes)
Turkey	Steaks	4–6
	Escalopes	2–3
Burgers	Commercial, 5 mm/¼ in thick	4–6
	Homemade, 1 cm/½ in thick	5–7
Sausages	Thick	6–8
	Chipolatas	3–4
Seafood	Fish fillets	2–4
	Fish steaks/cutlets	3–5
	Whole small, e.g. sardines	3–4
	Whole large, e.g. mackerel	5–6
	Raw large prawns (jumbo shrimp)	1–3
	Squid	2–4
	Scallops	1
Sandwiches		3–5
Vegetables	Asparagus	3–5
	Aubergines (eggplant), Courgettes (zucchini), Peppers (bell peppers)	4–6
	Broccoli	3–6
	Mushrooms, large, whole	3–4
	Onions, thick, sliced	4–7

CHEESE AND EGG GRILLS

You may not think that cheese and eggs are ideal for grilling but there are several simple but wonderful dishes here in which they are the integral part. One word of warning: beware of overcooking. Both cheese and eggs will continue to cook when they are taken out of the grill and if cooked too much they become leathery as they cool. You will find some other cheese recipes in the snack section, starting on page 93.

Cool, creamy goats' cheese, griddled just until it softens, then transferred to crispy toasted slices of French bread, served on a fresh salad, enhanced with cubes of sweet beetroot and juicy blueberries.

grilled goats' cheese croûtes with fresh blueberry salad

SERVES 4

A little sunflower oil
1 small bag of mixed salad leaves
2 baby beetroot (red beets), cut into
  small dice
1 small red onion, chopped
100 g/4 oz fresh blueberries
75 ml/5 tbsp olive oil

30 ml/2 tbsp raspberry vinegar
Salt and freshly ground black pepper
A good pinch of caster (superfine)
  sugar
4 slices of French bread
4 x 70 g/3 oz discs of firm goats'
  cheese

1   Oil the grill, then preheat it.

2   Tip the leaves into a large bowl. Add the beetroot, onion and blueberries.

3   Whisk 45 ml/3 tbsp of the olive oil with the vinegar, a little salt and pepper and the sugar.

4   Add to the salad and toss gently. Pile on four plates.

5   Brush the bread and the cheese on both sides with the remaining oil. Place the bread on the grill plates, close the lid and grill for 1 minute only until lightly toasted.

6   Open, top with the cheese, close the lid again and grill for 30 seconds until the cheese is just beginning to melt.

7   Transfer to the salads and serve straight away.

The savoury, crunchy coating adds delicious contrast to the melting richness of the Camembert. It is served with a sweet and fruity dressing on peppery wild rocket. Take care not to overcook the cheese or it will run everywhere!

crusty camembert
with celery and cranberry dressing

SERVES 4

8 individual portions of Camembert, chilled
1 large egg, beaten
1 x 85 g/3¹⁄₂ oz packet of parsley, thyme and lemon stuffing mix

FOR THE DRESSING:
30 ml/2 tbsp cranberry sauce
60 ml/4 tbsp olive oil, plus extra for brushing

15 ml/1 tbsp red wine vinegar
Salt and freshly ground black pepper
2 celery sticks, finely chopped
1 spring onion (scallion), finely chopped

TO SERVE:
1 small packet of wild rocket leaves

1   Dip the cheese in the egg, then the stuffing mix. Repeat the dipping until thoroughly coated. Chill until ready to cook.

2   Make the dressing. In a small bowl, whisk together the cranberry sauce, oil, vinegar and a little salt and pepper to taste. Stir in the celery and spring onion and chill until ready to serve.

3   When ready to cook, pile the rocket to one side of each of four small plates and spoon the dressing over.

4   Preheat the grill.

5   Brush the coated cheeses with oil and place on the grill. Cook on the open grill for 2 minutes, carefully turn over with a plastic spatula and cook the other side for 1¹⁄₂–2 minutes, pressing down lightly with a spatula until the cheese is just beginning to ooze.

6   Quickly transfer to the plates of salad and serve straight away.

Salty, firm cheese, marinated in garlic and oregano, wrapped in strong but sweet, wafer-thin ham and griddled until golden, then garnished with juicy cherry tomatoes and black olives. Hams such as Parma, Westphalian and Serrano are all suitable.

marinated halloumi cheese with dry-cured ham

SERVES 4

1 x 200 g/7 oz block of Halloumi
   cheese
8 thin slices of raw dry-cured ham
30 ml/2 tbsp olive oil
1 garlic clove, crushed
5 ml/1 tsp dried oregano

Freshly ground black pepper
12 cherry tomatoes, quartered
45 ml/3 tbsp sliced black olives

TO SERVE:
Greek bread

1   Cut the cheese into eight slices.

2   Wrap a slice of raw ham around each piece of cheese.

3   Place in a shallow dish and drizzle with a little olive oil, sprinkle with the garlic and oregano and add a good grinding of black pepper. Leave to marinate for at least 30 minutes.

4   Preheat the grill. Drain the parcels, pat dry and place on the grill. Close the lid and cook for 2 minutes until the ham and cheese are turning griddle-browned.

5   Mix the tomatoes and olives together. Put the ham-wrapped cheese on four plates with a pile of tomatoes and olives to one side.

6   Serve with Greek bread.

This delicious dish is perfect for breakfast, a light lunch or supper. Each fat, juicy tomato is stuffed with cooked ham and an egg and topped with cheese, then griddled until everything is cooked to perfection.

stuffed tomatoes
with cheese, ham and eggs

SERVES 4

4 large beefsteak tomatoes
A little olive oil
2 slices of ham, chopped
4 eggs
Freshly ground black pepper

50 g/2 oz/½ cup grated Cheddar
cheese

TO SERVE:
Granary bread

1   Preheat the grill.

2   Cut a slice off the rounded end (not the stalk end) of each tomato and scoop out the seeds. Brush inside and out with olive oil.

3   Put the ham into the tomatoes. Break an egg into each, season with pepper, then top with the cheese. Place on the grill.

4   If you have an adjustable lid, lower it gently so it is just touching the tomatoes and cook for 8 minutes. If not, close the lid so it is resting on the tomatoes but do not clip it shut. Cook for 5 minutes, then check to see how soft the tomatoes are. Continue to cook for 2–3 more minutes, checking frequently to make sure the tomatoes do not become too soft, or they will collapse under the weight of the unsupported lid. If necessary, finish cooking with the lid up for an extra minute or two.

5   Transfer the tomatoes to warm plates and serve with granary bread.

Jacket potatoes, scooped out, spicily seasoned and filled with an egg, then griddled until the egg sets to make a delicious light lunch or supper. Reserve the scooped-out potato for Potato and Corn Cakes with Cumin (see page 81) or to thicken soup.

spiced egg and potato nests

SERVES 4

4 fairly large potatoes, scrubbed
5 ml/1 tsp garam masala
Salt and freshly ground black pepper
25 g/1 oz/2 tbsp butter or
　margarine

4 eggs
30 ml/2 tbsp single (light) cream
30 ml/2 tbsp chopped fresh parsley
　or coriander (cilantro)

1　Prick the potatoes all over with a fork. Either boil in water for about 20 minutes until just tender or microwave for 12–15 minutes until soft when squeezed.

2　Drain, if necessary. When cool enough to handle, cut a slice off the top of each potato and reserve to use as lids. Scoop out about half of the potato into a bowl, leaving a wall about 3 mm/¹/₃ in thick.

3　Sprinkle the insides with the garam masala and a little salt and pepper. Dot with the butter or margarine.

4　Preheat the grill.

5　Break an egg into each potato and spoon the cream on top. Top with the lids. Place on the grill. If you have an adjustable grill, gently lower the lid so it rests lightly on the potatoes. If not, close the lid but do not press it down to clip it shut. Cook for 10 minutes until the eggs are set.

6　Sprinkle with the parsley or coriander and serve hot.

This tasty and nutritious bread is delicious on its own for a snack or served with grilled bacon or mushrooms for breakfast or lunch. Ring the changes by adding a sprinkling of chopped fresh herbs, such as chives or parsley, or a pinch of paprika.

eggy bread

SERVES 1–2

1 egg
10 ml/2 tsp milk
Salt and freshly ground black pepper

2 slices of bread
A little sunflower oil

1   Beat the egg and milk together with a sprinkling of salt and pepper in a shallow dish.

2   Cut the slices of bread in half and dip each half in the egg mixture until completely soaked.

3   Oil the grill well, then preheat it.

4   Drain the excess egg mixture off the slices of bread, then lay them on the hot plates. Close the lid and cook for 2–3 minutes until crisp and griddle-browned.

*Here's a fun recipe for toasted sandwiches with a difference –
the whole thing is soaked in beaten egg before grilling, then
cooked to make a golden, highly nutritious quick meal. Serve
with a salad for a complete meal.*

nutty cheese french toasts

MAKES 2

A little sunflower oil
100 g/4 oz/¹/₂ cup soft cheese with
    garlic and herbs
50 g/2 oz/¹/₂ cup roasted peanuts,
    chopped
30 ml/2 tbsp milk

Salt and freshly ground black pepper
30 ml/2 tbsp tomato relish or
    ketchup (catsup)
1 egg, beaten
4 slices of bread

1 Oil the grill, then preheat it.

2 Mix the cheese with the nuts and stir in 10 ml/2 tsp of the milk.
Season to taste.

3 Beat the egg with the remaining milk and a little salt and pepper
on a flat plate.

4 Spread two of the slices of bread with the cheese mixture. Spread
the others with the relish or ketchup. Sandwich together. Dip both
sides in the beaten egg. Drain well.

5 Place on the grill, close the lid and cook for 4 minutes until golden
and griddle-browned.

A nursery favourite: golden-toasted eggy bread, tossed in sugar and cinnamon and eaten warm. You could sandwich the slices together with mashed strawberries or raspberries or be really decadent and serve with whipped cream or crème fraîche too!

cinnamon french toast

SERVES 1

1 egg
10 ml/2 tsp milk
A pinch of salt
2 slices of bread
A little sunflower oil

30 ml/2 tbsp caster (superfine) sugar
5 ml/1 tsp ground cinnamon

TO SERVE:
Sliced fresh fruit (optional)

1 Beat the egg and milk together with a pinch of salt in a shallow dish.

2 Cut the slices of bread in half and dip each half in the egg mixture until completely soaked.

3 Oil the grill well, then preheat it. Drain the excess egg mixture off the slices of bread, then lay them on the hot plates. Close the lid and cook for 2–3 minutes until crisp and griddle-browned.

4 Mix the sugar and cinnamon together. Sprinkle over both sides of the griddle-browned bread to coat completely, then cut into pieces.

5 Serve hot, either plain or with sliced fresh fruit.

This is a low-fat alternative to the usual deep-fried recipe.
You will be thrilled to see hardly any fat oozes out of these –
especially if you use good-quality sausagemeat. The results are
delicious hot or cold.

griddled scotch eggs

SERVES 4

A little sunflower oil

450 g/1 lb pork sausagemeat

4 hard-boiled (hard-cooked) eggs, halved

2.5 ml/¹/₂ tsp dried sage

1 egg, beaten

50 g/2 oz/¹/₂ cup dried breadcrumbs

TO SERVE:

Pickles

1 Oil the grill, then preheat it.

2 Divide the sausagemeat into eight equal pieces. Flatten each one. Put half an egg in each piece, sprinkle with the sage and wrap the sausagemeat around each to cover completely and form flattish cakes. Dip in the beaten egg, then the breadcrumbs.

3 Place on the grill. If you have an adjustable lid, close it so it sits gently on the scotch eggs. If not, lower the lid and support the clip on a cork or other similar heat-resistant object, so that the lid just rests on the scotch eggs. Cook for 6–8 minutes. Alternatively, cook with the grill open for about 6–8 minutes on each side, pressing down lightly with a spatula, until griddle-browned and cooked through.

4 Serve hot or cold with pickles.

MEAT GRILLS

This is where your health grill really comes into its own. Just watch all the fat from sausages pouring into the drip tray — and you'll be surprised how much fat there is in the skin of a chicken portion! Remember that grilling doesn't tenderise meat, so always use top-quality cuts, sold as suitable for grilling. I guarantee, though, that the results of my exciting recipes will be tender, tasty, moist and utterly delicious.

Thick juicy steaks, marinated to ensure their tenderness, then griddled to your liking and served with a fresh, spicy salsa with the cooling addition of avocado. This classic combination is so easy but if you are really short of time, use ready-made salsa.

mexican spiced steaks
with fresh avocado salsa

SERVES 4

4 rump or sirloin steaks, about 175 g/
  6 oz each, trimmed of excess fat
45 ml/3 tbsp olive oil
10 ml/2 tsp lemon juice
5 ml/1 tsp dried chilli flakes
Freshly ground black pepper

FOR THE SALSA:
1 large ripe avocado
1 garlic clove, crushed
1 fresh green chilli, seeded and
  finely chopped

2 tomatoes, skinned, seeded and
  finely chopped
5 cm/2 in piece of cucumber,
  skinned and finely chopped
Salt

TO SERVE:
Potato wedges and a crisp green
  salad

1 Lay the steaks in a shallow dish. Mix 30 ml/2 tbsp of the oil with half the lemon juice, the chilli flakes and a good grinding of black pepper. Pour over the steaks and turn to coat completely. Leave to marinate for at least 1 hour.

2 Make the salsa. Halve and peel the avocado and remove the stone (pit). Cut the flesh into very small dice. Toss in the remaining oil and lemon juice. Add the remaining salsa ingredients, seasoning to taste with salt and pepper, then toss gently again. Chill until ready to serve.

3 Preheat the grill. Lift the meat out of the marinade, pat dry and lay it on the grill rack. Close the lid and grill for 2–6 minutes or until cooked to your liking.

4 Transfer to warm plates and spoon the salsa to one side.

5 Serve with potato wedges and a crisp green salad.

*Reminiscent of a holiday in Greece, these cubes of lamb
are marinated to impart flavour and succulence. If you don't
have fresh herbs, you can subsitute 10 ml/2 tsp of dried for
each one.*

sizzling lamb
with herbs and garlic

SERVES 4

450 g/1 lb lamb neck fillets
1 small red onion, grated
2 large garlic cloves, crushed
30 ml/2 tbsp olive oil
15 ml/1 tbsp lemon juice
30 ml/2 tbsp chopped fresh oregano
30 ml/2 tbsp chopped fresh mint
Salt and freshly ground black pepper

FOR THE DRESSING:
100 g/4 oz/½ cup fromage frais
75 ml/5 tbsp milk
5 ml/1 tsp lemon juice
30 ml/2 tbsp chopped fresh mint
Sprigs of fresh mint, for garnishing

TO SERVE:
Pitta breads, mixed salad leaves and
slices of cucumber

1   Cut the lamb into cubes, trimming off any fat or gristle.

2   Mix the onion, garlic, oil, lemon juice, herbs and a little salt and
    pepper in a shallow dish. Add the meat and toss with your hands
    to coat completely. Leave to marinate for at least 2 hours.

3   Mix the dressing ingredients together, season to taste and chill.

4   Preheat the grill. Remove the meat from the marinade, pat dry and
    place on the grill. Close the lid and cook for about 4 minutes or
    until slightly charred but still pink in the centre.

5   Split and open the pittas. Pack the meat, salad stuffs and dressing
    inside and serve.

Thin, tender slices of pork, stuffed with the favourite accompanying flavours of apple, onion and sage, griddled until golden and juicy and served with a very simple but delicious mushroom sauce.

stuffed pork rolls
with mushroom sauce

SERVES 4

4 thin slices of pork fillet

FOR THE STUFFING:
1 small onion, finely chopped
15 g/½ oz/1 tbsp butter or
   margarine
1 small eating (dessert) apple, finely
   chopped
5 ml/1 tsp dried sage
30 ml/2 tbsp chopped fresh parsley
50 g/2 oz/1 cup fresh breadcrumbs

Salt and freshly ground black pepper
1 egg yolk

FOR THE SAUCE:
1 x 170 g/6 oz/small can of
   creamed mushrooms
30 ml/2 tbsp milk
15 ml/1 tbsp chopped fresh parsley

TO SERVE:
New potatoes and French (green)
   beans

1   Place a slice of pork in a plastic bag, lay it on a work surface and beat with a rolling pin or meat mallet to flatten. Repeat with the remaining slices of meat.

2   Fry the onion in the butter or margarine for 2 minutes, stirring, to soften. Stir in the remaining stuffing ingredients. Spread the stuffing over the slices of meat and roll up. Tie with string or secure with cocktail sticks (toothpicks).

3   Make the sauce. Empty the creamed mushrooms into a saucepan and blend in the milk and parsley. Heat through, stirring.

4   Preheat the grill. Brush the pork rolls with the remaining oil and place on the grill. If you have an adjustable grill, lower the lid so it rests gently on top of the pork and grill for 6–7 minutes until cooked through and griddle-browned. If not, cook on the open grill for about 15 minutes, turning occasionally and pressing down lightly with a spatula.

5   Transfer to warm plates and spoon a little sauce over. Serve with new potatoes and French beans.

Turn humble sausagemeat into a gourmet experience with this delicious but easy-to-make dish. Don't try to cook these on a closed grill – the cheese will ooze out instead of being a gorgeous, gooey surprise when you cut the burgers open!

sausage burgers
stuffed with cheese, sage and onion

SERVES 4

2 Baby Bel cheeses
450 g/1 lb pork sausagemeat
1 small onion, finely chopped
4 sage leaves, finely chopped

TO SERVE:
Burger buns, mayonnaise and
 shredded lettuce

1 Preheat the grill. Remove the rind from the cheeses and cut into halves widthways.

2 Divide the sausagemeat into eight equal pieces and flatten each piece.

3 Put a cheese half on each of four sausage rounds. Top with the onion and sage, then the other sausage rounds and press the edges well together to seal.

4 Place on the grill. If you have an adjustable lid, lower it so it just rests on the sausage and grill for about 10 minutes until griddle-browned and cooked through. If not, cook on the open grill for about 10 minutes on each side, pressing down lightly with a spatula.

5 Split the burger buns and spread with mayonnaise. Add a sausage burger and some lettuce to each bun and serve.

These succulent thick slices of lamb, stuffed with fruity, salty and exotic ingredients, are also delicious served with the minted fromage frais dressing from the shish kebab recipe on page 38.

lamb fillets stuffed with apricots, feta and wild mushrooms

SERVES 4

450 g/1 lb lamb neck fillets
4 dried apricots, chopped
50 g/2 oz wild mushrooms, chopped
50 g/2 oz/½ cup crumbled feta
  cheese
15 ml/1 tbsp snipped fresh chives
Salt and freshly ground black pepper
60 ml/4 tbsp olive oil
30 ml/2 tbsp lemon juice
10 ml/2 tsp dried oregano

FOR THE DRESSING:
150 ml/¼ pt/⅔ cup plain Greek-
  style yoghurt
5 ml/1 tsp ground cumin
5 ml/1 tsp ground cinnamon
Grated zest and juice of ½ lemon
15 ml/1 tbsp clear honey

TO SERVE:
Couscous and a mixed salad

1 Trim any fat or gristle from the lamb.

2 Make a slit down the length of each fillet, not cutting right through, to form a pocket.

3 Mix the apricots, mushrooms, cheese, chives and a little salt and pepper together. Press into the cavities and tie securely with string.

4 Whisk the oil, lemon juice, oregano and a little salt and pepper together in a large shallow dish. Add the stuffed lamb and turn in the marinade. Leave to marinate for at least 2 hours, turning occasionally.

5 Mix the dressing ingredients together in a bowl and chill until ready to serve.

6 Preheat the grill.

7 Remove the meat from the marinade, and drain well. Place on the grill. If you have an adjustable grill, lower the lid gently so it just sits on the lamb and grill for about 8–10 minutes until well browned, tender and cooked to your liking. If not, cook on the open grill for about 8–10 minutes on each side, pressing down lightly with a spatula.

8 If liked, spoon off any fat from the drip tray (there may not be any), reserving the juices. Season the juices. Remove the string and cut the fillets into thick slices. Transfer to warm plates and spoon the meat juices over, if using.

9 Serve with couscous, the yoghurt dressing and a mixed salad.

A traditional meal with an original twist. It usually takes hours to bake these in the oven but your health grill will cook them in under 10 minutes, making a delicious midweek meal for all the family. Experiment with other fillings too.

grilled marrow rings
stuffed with herbed minced beef

SERVES 4

4 rings of young marrow, about
  2.5 cm/1 in thick, seeds removed
1 small onion, finely chopped
225 g/8 oz minced (ground) beef
25 ml/1½ tbsp plain (all-purpose)
  flour
450 ml/¾ pt/2 cups beef stock,
  made with 1 stock cube

2.5 ml/½ tsp dried mixed herbs
Salt and freshly ground black pepper
A little sunflower oil, for brushing

TO SERVE:
Creamed potatoes and broccoli

1 Cook the marrow rings in boiling, lightly salted water for
3 minutes. Drain thoroughly and pat dry on kitchen paper (paper towels).

2 Put the onion and meat in a saucepan and fry, stirring, until the grains of meat are separate and no longer pink. Stir in the flour.

3 Remove from the heat and gradually add the stock. Return to the heat, add the herbs, bring to the boil and cook for 2 minutes, stirring. Season to taste.

4 Preheat the grill. Brush the marrow rings with oil and place on the grill. Using a draining spoon, fill the centres with the meat, reserving most of the gravy.

5 Close the lid and cook for 7 minutes until the marrow is just tender and the surface is griddle-browned. Meanwhile, reheat the gravy.

6 Transfer the marrow to warm plates with a spatula. Pour any juices in the drip tray back into the gravy, then spoon it over the marrow.

7 Serve with creamed potatoes and broccoli.

Fast-food burgers aren't a patch on these tasty, succulent patties. Transfer them to giant buns, if you like, and top them with every relish and pickle you can think of for a mighty meal in minutes.

jumbo beefburgers
with sweet dill pickle relish

SERVES 4

FOR THE BURGERS:
450 g/1 lb minced (ground) steak
1 onion, finely chopped
1 garlic clove, crushed
5 ml/1 tsp tomato purée (paste)
5 ml/1 tsp Dijon mustard
5 ml/1 tsp Worcestershire sauce
5 ml/1 tsp dried mixed herbs
Salt and freshly ground black pepper
1 egg, beaten

FOR THE RELISH:
2 dill-pickled cucumbers, finely
   chopped
1 small green (bell) pepper, finely
   chopped
2 spring onions (scallions), finely
   chopped
10 ml/2 tsp clear honey
15 ml/1 tbsp of the dill pickle
   vinegar
A little sunflower oil

TO SERVE:
Sauté potatoes and a large mixed
   salad

1 Mix all the burger ingredients thoroughly together. Shape into four cakes and chill until ready to cook.

2 Mix the relish ingredients together and chill.

3 Oil the grill, then preheat it. Put the burgers on the grill. If you have an adjustable lid, lower it so it sits lightly on the burgers and cook for about 5 minutes or until cooked through and griddle-browned. If not, cook on the open grill for about 5 minutes on each side, pressing down lightly with a spatula.

4 Serve the burgers hot, with the relish, sauté potatoes and a large mixed salad.

A touch of the Middle East here but with an original twist – nuts and celery, to add texture and flavour. The mint fromage frais makes a nice change from a yoghurt dressing but you could also serve them with a barbecue sauce.

crunchy shish kebabs
with cool mint fromage frais

SERVES 4

FOR THE KEBABS:
450 g/1 lb minced (ground) beef, lamb or pork
40 g/1½ oz/¾ cup fresh white breadcrumbs
1 small onion, finely chopped
1 garlic clove, crushed
1 celery stick, finely chopped
50 g/2 oz/½ cup peanuts, chopped
5 ml/1 tsp ground cumin
5 ml/1 tsp dried oregano
Salt and freshly ground black pepper
1 egg, beaten

FOR THE DRESSING:
100 g/4 oz/½ cup fromage frais
10 ml/2 tsp bottled garden mint
1 small garlic clove, crushed
A good pinch of caster (superfine) sugar
A little olive oil, for brushing
Wedges of lemon, for garnishing

TO SERVE:
Warm pitta breads and a large mixed salad

1 Mix all the kebab ingredients together in a large bowl. Shape into sausages around eight wooden skewers that have been soaked in cold water. Chill until ready to cook.

2 Mix the dressing ingredients together and chill.

3 Preheat the grill. Brush the kebabs with a little oil and place on the grill. If you have an adjustable grill, close the lid so it rests gently on top of the kebabs and grill for about 5 minutes until cooked through and griddle-browned. If not, cook on the open grill for about 5 minutes on each side.

4 Garnish with wedges of lemon and serve with the dressing, warm pitta breads and a large salad.

Steak is sensational when cooked on your health grill. Here it is cut into cubes, marinated and griddled quickly to succulent perfection. The mustard dip adds a nice touch but you could serve them with griddled mushrooms and tomatoes if you like.

griddled fillet steak cubes with mustard dip

SERVES 4

450 g/1 lb fillet steak, cut into cubes
30 ml/2 tbsp olive oil
5 ml/1 tsp lemon juice
5 ml/1 tsp black mustard seeds
Salt and freshly ground black pepper

FOR THE DIP:
75 ml/5 tbsp mayonnaise
75 ml/5 tbsp crème fraîche
30 ml/2 tbsp grainy mustard

TO SERVE:
French bread and a crisp green salad

1   Mix the steak with the oil, lemon juice, mustard seeds and a little salt and pepper. Leave to marinate for at least 30 minutes.

2   Mix the dip ingredients together, spoon into small pots and chill until ready to serve.

3   Preheat the grill. Lift the cubes of steak out of the marinade, drain well and lay on the grill. Close the lid and cook for 2–6 minutes according to how you like your steak. Transfer the steak to warm plates and put a small pot of dip on each plate.

4   Serve with French bread and a crisp green salad.

A touch of luxury in this recipe – thick steaks stuffed with smooth pâté and flavoured with a hint of spice, then wrapped in bacon for added succulence and flavour. The results are fantastic – a real treat for the family or perfect to serve guests.

carpet bag steaks

SERVES 4

4 fillet or thick rump steaks
A few drops of Tabasco sauce
A few drops of Worcestershire sauce
100 g/4 oz coarse liver pâté with
  mushrooms
15 ml/1 tbsp sunflower oil
Freshly ground black pepper

8 rashers (slices) of streaky bacon,
  rinded
Tomato halves and sprigs of fresh
  parsley, for garnishing

TO SERVE:
Jacket potatoes, mushrooms and
  mangetout (snow peas)

1   Make a deep slit in the side of each steak to form a pocket.

2   Sprinkle a few drops each of the Tabasco and Worcestershire sauces inside the pockets, then pack with the pâté.

3   Brush each steak on both sides with oil and season with pepper. Stretch each bacon rasher with the back of a knife. Wrap two round each steak and secure with cocktail sticks (toothpicks), if necessary. Chill until ready to cook.

4   Preheat the grill. Put the steaks on the grill. If you have an adjustable grill, lower the lid so it sits lightly on the steaks (make sure the cocktails sticks are not in the way, if used) and cook for 3–8 minutes, until cooked to your liking. If not, cook on the open grill for 3–8 minutes on each side, pressing down lightly with a spatula.

5   Transfer to warm plates and remove the cocktail sticks, if used. Garnish with tomato halves and sprigs of fresh parsley.

6   Serve with jacket potatoes, mushrooms and mangetout.

Gammon is quick-cooking and nearly always tender but when lightly caramelised it has depth of flavour as well as succulence. You can serve it with griddled slices of pineapple, kiwi fruit or apple, if you like.

caramelised gammon

SERVES 2

2 gammon steaks
15 ml/1 tbsp sunflower oil
5 ml/1 tsp light brown sugar
2.5 ml/½ tsp dried sage
Sprigs of fresh parsley, for
  garnishing

TO SERVE:
Mustard, sauté potatoes and French
  (green) beans

1 Preheat the grill.

2 Snip the gammon steaks all round with scissors to stop them curling during cooking. Brush with the oil and sprinkle on both sides with the sugar and sage.

3 Lay the gammon on the grill (if very large you may have to cook one at a time). Close the lid and cook for 3–6 minutes, depending on thickness, until griddle-browned and cooked through.

4 Transfer the gammon to warm plates and garnish with sprigs of fresh parsley.

5 Serve with mustard, sauté potatoes and French beans.

Liver is never better than when quickly griddled. The outside becomes faintly crusty if dusted in seasoned flour first, but the centre remains soft and tender. As always when cooking liver, do take care not to overcook it.

peppered liver and onions

SERVES 4

2 Spanish onions, halved and cut into slices
45–60 ml/3–4 tbsp sunflower oil
45 ml/3 tbsp plain (all-purpose) flour
A good pinch of salt
30 ml/2 tbsp coarsely ground black peppercorns

350 g/12 oz lamb's liver, cut into thin slices

TO SERVE:
Creamed potatoes and cauliflower cheese

1   Preheat the grill.

2   Brush the onion slices with oil on both sides. Mix the flour with the salt. Toss the onions in the flour, reserving the remainder. Place on the grill, close the lid and cook for about 6 minutes until griddle-striped and tender. Remove from the grill and keep warm.

3   Meanwhile, mix the remaining flour with the pepper on a plate. Brush the liver with more of the oil, then dip in the flour and pepper to coat completely. Oil the grill and reheat it.

4   Lay the liver on the grill, close and cook for 1–2 minutes until griddle-browned but still pink in the middle.

5   Serve the liver and onions with creamed potatoes and cauliflower cheese.

Another classic made easy. Instead of frying the bread, you griddle it before you cook the steaks. The croûtes are then spread with pâté, topped with the tender, juicy fillet steak and bathed in a rich, red wine sauce.

tournedos rossini

SERVES 4

150 ml/¼ pt/⅔ cup red wine
60 ml/4 tbsp water
1 bouquet garni sachet
15 ml/1 tbsp dried minced (ground) onion
30 ml/2 tbsp tomato purée (paste)
5 ml/1 tsp caster (superfine) sugar
15 ml/1 tbsp brandy
Salt and freshly ground black pepper

4 slices of bread
A little olive oil
4 fillet steaks
50 g/2 oz smooth liver pâté
A little chopped fresh parsley, for garnishing

TO SERVE:
Sauté potatoes and French (green) beans

1   Put the wine, water, bouquet garni, onion, tomato purée and sugar in a saucepan. Bring to the boil, reduce the heat and simmer for 5 minutes, stirring until slightly thickened. Add the brandy and season to taste.

2   Preheat the grill.

3   Cut a round out of each slice of bread, making it as large as possible. Brush with oil. Place on the grill, close the lid and cook for 3 minutes. Remove.

4   Reheat the grill, brush the steaks with oil, then place on the grill. If you have an adjustable grill, lower the lid so it sits gently on top of the steaks and cook for 3–8 minutes, depending on how you like your steak. If not, cook on the open grill for 3–8 minutes on each side, pressing down lightly with a spatula.

5   Meanwhile, spread the toasted bread with the pâté and place on warm plates. Reheat the sauce. Place a steak on each slice of toast and pâté. Remove the bouquet garni from the sauce and spoon the sauce over the steaks. Garnish with a little chopped fresh parsley.

6   Serve with sauté potatoes and French beans.

Succulent, tangy, slightly fiery and very fragrant, these tender hunks of meat are extremely moist and delicious. The apple slices help to offset the richness and the suggestion of creamed parsnips as an accompaniment is a real winner.

marinated spiced pork fillet with apples

SERVES 4

10 ml/2 tsp cumin seeds, crushed
15 ml/1 tbsp olive oil, plus extra for brushing
15 ml/1 tbsp balsamic vinegar
15 ml/1 tbsp soy sauce
90 ml/6 tbsp dry white wine
1 small red chilli, seeded and finely chopped
450 g/1 lb pork tenderloin, trimmed of any fat or sinews

2 Golden Delicious apples
150 ml/¼ pt/⅔ cup beef stock, made with ½ stock cube
Salt and freshly ground black pepper
Sprigs of fresh parsley, for garnishing

TO SERVE:
Creamed parsnips and French (green) beans

1   Whisk the cumin, oil, vinegar, soy sauce, wine and chilli together in a shallow dish. Add the pork and turn to coat completely. Cover and chill for several hours – overnight if possible – turning occasionally.

2   Preheat the grill. Drain the pork well from the marinade and lay it on the grill. Close the lid and cook for about 10–12 minutes until griddle-browned and the meat gives easily when a skewer is inserted in the thickest part. Alternatively, cook on the open grill for about 20 minutes, turning occasionally. Wrap in foil and leave to rest for at least 5 minutes before cutting.

3   Cut the tops and bases off the apples and cut each one into four slices. Cut out the cores. Brush with a little oil. Place on the grill, close the lid and cook for 5 minutes.

4   Meanwhile, strain the remaining marinade into a small saucepan. Add the stock and boil rapidly for several minutes, stirring, until reduced by half. Taste and season, if necessary.

5   Cut the pork into thick slices, lay them on warm plates and spoon the sauce over. Garnish with the apple rings and sprigs of fresh parsley.

6   Serve with creamed parsnips and French beans.

Rich, tender and very tasty, these ribs need marinating for a while before cooking to impart their true flavour. Serve them as a starter or cook more in batches for a main meal with egg fried rice and stir-fried vegetables.

chinese mandarin spareribs

SERVES 4

8 pork spareribs
1 x 300 g/11 oz/medium can of
    mandarin oranges in natural juice,
    drained
45 ml/3 tbsp balsamic vinegar
30 ml/2 tbsp soy sauce

1 large garlic clove, crushed
5 ml/1 tsp clear honey
2.5 ml/^{1}/$_2$ tsp Chinese five-spice
    powder
A little sunflower oil

1   Place the ribs in a large saucepan. Cover with water, bring to the boil, reduce the heat and simmer gently for 1 hour. Drain and place in a shallow dish.

2   Purée the mandarins in a blender or food processor with the vinegar, soy sauce, garlic, honey and five-spice powder. Pour the mixture over the ribs and turn to coat completely. Leave to marinate for several hours, turning once or twice.

3   Oil the grill, then preheat it. Turn down to medium heat. Drain the ribs thoroughly and arrange on the grill. Close the grill as far as possible, depending on the thickness, and cook for about 15 minutes until a rich brown, turning and rearranging once or twice so that different parts of the ribs touch the grill.

4   Meanwhile, tip the remaining marinade into a small saucepan. Bring to the boil and simmer until syrupy.

5   Transfer the cooked ribs to a serving dish. Pour the sauce over, toss to coat and serve.

The combination of seafood with steak is a great Californian favourite. Here both are grilled to perfection and served with a piquant mayonnaise – an exciting change from the more usual tartare sauce.

surf 'n' turf with mustard and caperberry mayonnaise

SERVES 4

4 fillet steaks, about 150 g/5 oz
  each
45 ml/3 tbsp sunflower oil
15 ml/1 tbsp steak seasoning
12 raw king prawns (jumbo shrimp),
  shelled but tails left on, thawed if
  frozen
Juice of ½ lemon
90 ml/6 tbsp mayonnaise

45 ml/3 tbsp crème fraîche
15 ml/1 tbsp Dijon mustard
15 ml/1 tbsp chopped fresh parsley
Freshly ground black pepper
12 pickled caperberries

TO SERVE:
Baby new potatoes in their skins and
  a mixed salad

1 Brush the steaks with some of the oil and dust liberally with the steak seasoning.

2 Lay the prawns in a shallow dish and sprinkle with the lemon juice and the remaining oil. Toss with your hands to coat completely.

3 Mix together all the remaining ingredients except the caperberries. Chop four caperberries and add to the mayonnaise. Chill until ready to serve.

4 Preheat the grill. Lay the steaks on the grill, close the lid and cook for 3–8 minutes or until cooked to your liking. Remove from the grill and keep warm.

5 Reheat the grill. Drain the prawns well, lay them on the grill, close the lid and cook for 2 minutes only, until just pink.

6 Transfer the steaks and prawns to warm plates and garnish each plate with 2 caperberries.

7 Serve with the mustard mayonnaise, baby new potatoes in their skins and a mixed salad.

POULTRY
GRILLS

Pieces of chicken, turkey and duck all grill beautifully but if you are using skinless portions, always make sure you oil them well or marinate them before grilling or they will be tough and dry on the outside once they are cooked through. Chicken and turkey should always be thoroughly cooked, although duck breasts can be served slightly pink in the centre and, indeed, they are more moist and tender that way.

This simple dish has an exciting combination of flavours and textures and a definite Mediterranean influence. For added flavour, toss the tagliatelle in a tomato pasta sauce before serving with a green salad instead of the tomato one I've suggested.

pancetta-wrapped chicken
with olive, basil and pine nut dressing

SERVES 4

4 skinless chicken breasts
8 rashers (slices) of pancetta
A little olive oil

FOR THE DRESSING:
50 g/2 oz/¹/₂ cup stoned (pitted)
  green olives
12 large fresh basil leaves

1 garlic clove
50 g/2 oz/¹/₂ cup pine nuts
90 ml/6 tbsp olive oil
Lemon juice, to taste
Freshly ground black pepper

TO SERVE:
Tagliatelle and a tomato salad

1   Wrap the chicken in the pancetta, then brush all over with olive oil.

2   Put the olives, basil, garlic and pine nuts in a blender or food processor and run the machine to chop them finely, stopping and scraping down the sides every so often. Add the measured oil in a thin trickle, running the machine all the time. Season to taste with lemon juice and pepper.

3   Preheat the grill.

4   Lay the chicken on the grill, close the lid and cook for 5–6 minutes until griddle-browned and cooked through. Transfer to warm plates and spoon a little of the dressing over.

5   Serve with tagliatelle and a tomato salad.

There is no doubt that marinating then griddling chicken produces moist and meltingly tender results. Here the added flavours of lemon, garlic and herbs make the dish irresistible hot or cold.

marinated chicken legs with garlic, lemon and thyme

SERVES 4

12 chicken legs
45 ml/3 tbsp olive oil
Finely grated zest and juice of
  1 small lemon
1 garlic clove, crushed

1 small onion, sliced and separated
  into rings
15 ml/1 tbsp chopped fresh
  (or 5 ml/1 tsp dried) thyme
Freshly ground black pepper
A little coarse sea salt (optional)

1 Wipe the chicken legs with kitchen paper (paper towels). Make several slashes in the flesh of each leg.

2 Mix all the remaining ingredients except the coarse sea salt together in a shallow dish, just large enough to take the legs in one layer. Put the chicken legs in the dish and turn them over in the marinade to coat completely. Cover and chill for at least 3 hours, turning occasionally.

3 Preheat the grill. Drain the chicken legs well and place on the grill. Close the lid. Cook for about 10 minutes or until griddle-browned and cooked through.

4 Sprinkle with a little coarse sea salt, if liked, and serve hot or cold.

Tandoori dishes are traditionally cooked in a clay oven, but your health grill will render the meat equally succulent. You can use chicken leg portions if you prefer, but remove the skin and cook them for a minute or two more.

tandoori-style chicken breasts with minted raita

SERVES 4

4 skinned chicken breasts

FOR THE TANDOORI MARINADE:
90 ml/6 tbsp plain yoghurt
1 garlic clove, crushed
5 ml/1 tsp grated fresh root ginger
15 ml/1 tbsp tandoori powder

FOR THE RAITA:
90 ml/6 tbsp thick plain yoghurt

5 cm/2 in piece of cucumber, finely diced
10 ml/2 tsp dried mint
Salt and freshly ground black pepper
Shredded lettuce, wedges of lemon and onion rings, for garnishing

TO SERVE:
Naan bread

1   Make several slashes in the chicken breasts with a sharp knife.

2   Mix all the tandoori ingredients together in a shallow dish and add the chicken. Turn over to coat completely. Leave to marinate for several hours.

3   Meanwhile, mix the raita ingredients together and season with salt and pepper.

4   Preheat the grill. Lift the chicken out of the marinade and drain well. Place on the grill, close the lid and cook for 5–6 minutes until cooked through and griddle-browned.

5   Transfer to plates, garnish with shredded lettuce, wedges of lemon and onion rings, and serve with naan bread and the raita.

If your poussins are large, cook them one at a time on an adjustable grill for the time given below. Or, place on the open grill for 10–15 minutes each side, brushing with the honey half way through and turning skin-sides down for the last 5 minutes.

spatchcocked poussins with pesto

SERVES 2 OR 4

2 poussins (Cornish hens)
60 ml/4 tbsp pesto
30 ml/2 tbsp olive oil
Freshly ground black pepper

15 ml/1 tbsp clear honey

TO SERVE:
Focaccia with olives and a rocket and avocado salad

1 To spatchcock the poussins, cut through both sides of the backbone from the parson's nose to the neck with poultry shears or a sharp kitchen knife. Remove the backbone. Turn the birds over, flatten out by pressing the breastbone down and fold the drumsticks towards the centre.

2 From the neck end, carefully ease the skin away from the breast. Spoon half the pesto under the skin of each bird. Brush the skin all over with some of the oil and sprinkle with pepper.

3 Oil the grill, then preheat it. Put the poussins on the grill. Close the lid and cook for 8 minutes. Open and brush with honey. Close the lid again and cook for a further 3–5 minutes until griddle-browned and cooked through.

4 Transfer to warm plates. Cut in half, if liked. Spoon any fat off the juices in the drip tray, then spoon the juices over the chicken.

5 Serve with focaccia with olives and a rocket and avocado salad.

The bacon helps to keep the chicken moist and juicy and the rosemary adds a fabulous flavour to the stuffing. It's quick to prepare, too, but if you have time, try serving it with Mushroom Sauce (see page 32) or Fresh Tomato Sauce (see page 83).

rosemary-stuffed chicken in bacon

SERVES 4

50 g/2 oz/1 cup fresh breadcrumbs
30 ml/2 tbsp chopped fresh
  rosemary
15 ml/1 tbsp chopped fresh parsley
1 small garlic clove, crushed
Salt and freshly ground black pepper
1 egg, beaten
4 skinless chicken breasts

4 rashers (slices) of back bacon
30 ml/2 tbsp olive oil
Sprigs of fresh rosemary,
  for garnishing

TO SERVE:
Sauté potatoes and mangetout
(snow peas)

1 Mix the breadcrumbs with the rosemary, parsley, garlic and a little salt and pepper. Add the beaten egg to bind and leave to stand for at least 15 minutes.

2 Make a slit in the side of each chicken breast and fill with the stuffing.

3 Stretch the bacon rashers with the back of a knife, then wrap one around each chicken breast.

4 Preheat the grill. Brush the chicken all over with oil. Place on the grill, close the lid and cook for 6–8 minutes until cooked through and griddle-browned.

5 Garnish with sprigs of rosemary, then serve with sauté potatoes and mangetout.

A long-term favourite, chicken wings cook quickly on your health grill. Succulent wings coated in a sweet, spicy sauce make a delicious snack, starter or buffet dish. You may need to cook them in two batches if they are large.

barbecued chicken wings

SERVES 4

1 garlic clove, crushed
15 ml/1 tbsp sunflower oil,
   plus extra for brushing
15 ml/1 tbsp clear honey
5 ml/1 tsp made English mustard

15 ml/1 tbsp tomato ketchup
   (catsup)
30 ml/2 tbsp red wine vinegar
10 ml/2 tsp Worcestershire sauce
15 ml/1 tbsp soy sauce
16 chicken wings

1 Blend together all the ingredients except the chicken wings.

2 Cut the wing tips off the chicken wings at the first joint and discard.

3 Add the chicken wings to the marinade, toss well and leave in a cool place for at least 1 hour.

4 Oil the grill, then preheat it.

5 Lift the chicken out of the marinade, draining well. Place the wings on the grill and close the lid. Cook for about 10 minutes until cooked through and tender.

6 Serve hot or cold.

This is a lovely variation on a Tex Mex theme: griddled chicken, sliced and served with griddled peppers, moistened with crème fraîche and tomato relish and wrapped in flour tortillas for easy eating.

chicken and roast vegetable fajitas

SERVES 4

4 skinless chicken breasts
1 large garlic clove, crushed
Finely grated zest and juice of 1 lime
1 red chilli, seeded and finely chopped
15 ml/1 tbsp paprika
5 ml/1 tsp dried oregano
2.5 ml/½ tsp ground cumin
1.5 ml/¼ tsp ground cinnamon
60 ml/4 tbsp olive oil

Salt and freshly ground black pepper
2 red (bell) peppers, cut into thin strips
1 green pepper, cut into thin strips
2 red onions, sliced

TO SERVE:
12 flour tortillas, tomato or chilli relish, crème fraîche and iceberg lettuce, finely shredded

1   Wipe the chicken and slash in several places with a sharp knife. Place in a shallow dish.

2   Mix together the garlic, lime zest and juice, chilli, paprika, oregano, cumin and cinnamon with 30 ml/2 tbsp of the oil. Season lightly with salt and pepper and pour over the chicken. Turn to coat completely. Cover and leave to marinate for at least 1 hour.

3   Mix the peppers and onions with the remaining oil.

4   Preheat the grill. Drain the chicken well, lay it on the grill, close the lid and cook for 6–8 minutes or until the chicken is cooked through. Remove, wrap in foil and keep warm.

5   Reheat the grill, add the peppers and onions, close the lid and cook for about 6 minutes until softened and slightly charred in places.

6   Meanwhile, warm the tortillas.

7   Carve the chicken breasts into thin slices.

8   To serve, spread the tortillas with a little relish and add the vegetables and chicken. Top with a little crème fraîche and shredded lettuce, roll up and eat in your fingers.

A complete and delicious oriental-style meal, this recipe makes your health grill work in conjunction with your normal cooker. The grill cooks the kebabs perfectly while you quickly stir-fry a selection of crisp vegetables.

teryaki kebabs on vegetable stir-fry

SERVES 4

30 ml/2 tbsp soy sauce
30 ml/2 tbsp medium-dry sherry
1 garlic clove, crushed
2.5 ml/1/2 tsp grated fresh root
    ginger
10 ml/2 tsp clear honey
4 skinless chicken breasts, cut into
    cubes
A little sunflower oil

FOR THE STIR-FRY:
1 x 350 g/12 oz packet of prepared
    fresh stir-fry vegetables, including
    beansprouts
15 ml/1 tbsp soy sauce

1   Mix the soy sauce with the sherry, garlic, ginger and honey.

2   Add the chicken cubes and toss well. Leave in a cool place to marinate for at least 2 hours.

3   Oil the grill, then preheat it.

4   Drain the chicken well from the marinade, then thread on wooden skewers that have been soaked in cold water. Place on the grill and close the lid. Cook for about 6 minutes or until tender and cooked through.

5   Meanwhile, heat a little oil in a frying pan or wok. Add the vegetables and stir-fry for about 3 minutes. Add any remaining marinade and the extra soy sauce and toss well. Pile on plates and top with the kebabs.

Juicy, tender turkey cakes with everyone's favourite accompaniment, cranberry sauce, inside, all served on a crisp, grilled slice of bread, instead of the more usual burger bun. You can use 5 ml/1 tsp dried thyme if you have no fresh.

turkey patties with cranberry

SERVES 4

450 g/1 lb minced (ground) turkey
1 small onion, finely chopped
30 ml/2 tbsp chopped fresh parsley
15 ml/1 tbsp chopped fresh thyme
45 ml/3 tbsp fresh breadcrumbs
Finely grated zest of 1 lime
1 egg, beaten

Salt and freshly ground black pepper
30 ml/2 tbsp cranberry sauce
4 slices of wholemeal bread
Butter or margarine, for spreading

TO SERVE
A grated carrot salad

1   Mix the turkey with the onion, herbs, breadcrumbs, lime zest, egg and a little salt and pepper. Divide into eight equal pieces and flatten into rounds.

2   Spoon the cranberry sauce into the centres of four of the rounds. Top with the remaining rounds and press the edges well together to seal.

3   Preheat the grill.

4   Cut rounds out of the slices of bread, using a large biscuit (cookie) cutter. Spread lightly on both sides with butter or margarine. Place on the grill, close and cook for 1–2 minutes until griddle-browned. Remove from the grill and keep warm.

5   Put the patties on the grill. If you have an adjustable grill, lower the lid so it sits lightly on the patties and grill for 10 minutes or until cooked through and griddle-browned. If not, cook on the open grill for 10 minutes on each side, pressing down lightly with a spatula. Transfer to the croûtes of bread on warm plates.

6   Serve with a grated carrot salad.

I often coat turkey steaks in crumbs of one sort or another because they just work so well together. I was thrilled that they were so successful on the health grill – the results are crunchy, tender and succulent all at the same time!

turkey steaks with herb and walnut crust

SERVES 4

4 turkey steaks
1 x 85 g/3½ oz packet of parsley
   and thyme stuffing mix
50 g/2 oz/½ cup finely chopped
   walnuts
1 egg, beaten

A little sunflower oil
Wedges of lemon and sprigs of
   watercress, for garnishing

TO SERVE:
Redcurrant jelly (clear conserve),
   creamed potatoes and peas

1   Put each steak in a plastic bag, lay it on a work surface and beat just a little to tenderise. Don't make them too thin.

2   Mix together the stuffing mix and the chopped walnuts.

3   Dip each steak in the beaten egg, then the stuffing, to coat completely.

4   Oil the grill, then preheat it. Drizzle the steaks with a little oil too. Lay the steaks on the grill, close the lid and cook for 4 minutes until griddle-browned and cooked through.

5   Transfer to warm plates, garnish with wedges of lemon and sprigs of watercress.

6   Serve with redcurrant jelly, creamed potatoes and peas.

Tender duck, full of fragrant flavour, with a slightly crispy skin. To make the garnish, make six cuts from the rounded end of each tomato to the stalk, without slicing right through. Gently open up the points to make 'flowers'.

duck with ginger and hoisin sauce

SERVES 4

30 ml/2 tbsp sunflower oil
1 garlic clove, crushed
5 ml/1 tsp grated fresh root ginger
30 ml/2 tbsp soy sauce
2.5 ml/¹/₂ tsp Chinese five-spice
powder

4 duck leg portions
Cherry tomatoes and whole chive
stalks, for garnishing

TO SERVE:
Hoisin sauce, egg fried rice and a
beansprout salad

1 Mix the oil with the garlic, ginger, soy sauce and five-spice powder in a shallow dish. Add the duck and turn to coat the pieces completely. Leave to marinate for at least 2 hours.

2 Preheat the grill. Drain the portions well, then lay them on the grill (you may have to do them two at a time if they are large), close the lid and cook for 10 minutes or until griddle-browned and tender. Transfer to warm plates, garnish with cherry tomato 'flowers' and whole chive stalks.

3 Serve with hoisin sauce, egg fried rice and a beansprout salad.

FISH
GRILLS

Fish is always quick to cook so it makes almost instant meals on a health grill! You can enjoy the simple pleasure of a grilled salmon steak or the more exotic flavours of swordfish, red mullet or squid. All these recipes make fabulous eating and will encourage you to put fish on the menu much more often. Two tips: always take great care not to overcook fish or it will be dry and hard. And remember that all frozen seafood is best thawed completely before cooking on your grill.

It's worth taking the trouble to open out the squid first so it cooks quickly and evenly – that way it remains really tender. You can experiment with much larger squid if you can get it – just cook it for a little longer until tender.

garlic-marinated grilled baby squid with lemon and parsley

SERVES 4

12 baby squid, cleaned
45 ml/3 tbsp olive oil
1 large garlic clove, crushed
10 ml/2 tsp lemon juice
Salt and freshly ground black pepper

45 ml/3 tbsp chopped fresh parsley
Wedges of lemon, for garnishing

TO SERVE:
Crusty bread

1 Remove the tentacles from inside the squid, if necessary. Trim them and discard the rest of the head parts. Rinse the squid and dry on kitchen paper (paper towels). Split open and lay flat. Put them in a shallow dish with the tentacles and add 15 ml/1 tbsp of the oil, the garlic, lemon juice and a little salt and pepper. Leave to marinate for at least 1 hour.

2 Preheat the grill. Lift the squid out of the marinade, pat dry and lay it flat on the grill. Close the lid and cook for 4 minutes. Transfer to warm plates.

3 Trickle the remaining oil over and sprinkle with the parsley. Garnish with wedges of lemon.

4 Serve with crusty bread.

This warm salad of quickly seared salmon on sweet baby potatoes, cool cucumber and crispy leaves, all bathed in a creamy, dill-flavoured dressing, makes a fabulous, summery dish for any occasion. Try it with trout or mackerel fillets too.

warm salmon and potato salad with fresh dill dressing

SERVES 4

225 g/8 oz baby new potatoes
4 thick middle salmon steaks
15 ml/1 tbsp sunflower oil
150 ml/¹/₄ pt/²/₃ cup crème fraîche
75 ml/5 tbsp milk
15 ml/1 tbsp lemon juice

30 ml/2 tbsp chopped fresh dill (dill weed)
5 ml/1 tsp caster (superfine) sugar
Salt and freshly ground black pepper
1 small packet of mixed salad leaves
¹/₄ cucumber, diced

1 Cook the potatoes in boiling, lightly salted water until tender, then drain.

2 Preheat the grill.

3 Brush the fish with oil and lay them on the grill. If you have an adjustable grill, lower the lid until it rests gently on top of the fish and cook for 4–5 minutes until just cooked through. If not, cook on the open grill for 4–5 minutes on each side, pressing down lightly with a spatula.

4 Meanwhile, whisk the crème fraîche and milk with the lemon juice, dill and sugar. Season with salt and pepper.

5 Pile the salad leaves on plates and scatter the potatoes and diced cucumber over.

6 Lay a salmon steak on top of each pile and spoon the dressing over.

Cod steaks, topped with flavoursome vegetables, served on richly browned slices of parsnip with a piquant but creamy sauce – this is an inspired combination! Serve it with some fresh green peas or a green vegetable for a delicious meal.

griddled cod with parsnip slices and rainbow peppercorn sauce

SERVES 4

15 g/¹/₂ oz/1 tbsp butter or
   margarine
1 celery stick, cut into matchsticks
1 small carrot, cut into matchsticks
175 ml/6 fl oz/³/₄ cup dry cider
15 ml/1 tbsp cornflour (cornstarch)
150 ml/¹/₄ pt/²/₃ cup single (light)
   cream
15 ml/1 tbsp pickled rainbow
   (Bristol Blend) peppercorns

Salt and freshly ground black pepper
1 large parsnip, trimmed and cut
   lengthways into 4 slices
30 ml/2 tbsp sunflower oil
4 pieces of cod fillet,
   about 175 g/6 oz each

TO SERVE:
Peas

1 Make the sauce. Heat the butter or margarine in a small saucepan. Add the celery and carrot and cook, stirring, for 1 minute to soften slightly. Add the cider, bring to the boil, cover, turn down the heat and simmer for 5 minutes or until the vegetables are tender.

2 Lift the vegetables out of the liquid, reserve and keep warm.

3 Blend the cornflour with 30 ml/2 tbsp of cold water and stir into the pan. Bring to the boil and cook for 1 minute. Stir in the cream and peppercorns. Season lightly with salt.

4 Preheat the grill.

5 Brush the slices of parsnip with oil on both sides. Brush the fish with oil on both sides, then season with black pepper.

6 Lay the parsnips on the grill. Close the lid and cook for 5–6 minutes or until well browned and cooked through. Remove and keep warm. Put the fish on the grill, close the lid and cook for 2–4 minutes until cooked through.

7 Meanwhile, reheat the sauce.

8 Transfer the parsnips slices to warm plates. Top with the cod, then the celery and carrot sticks and spoon the sauce over.

9 Serve with peas.

The trick with scallops is not to overcook them. They are expensive but truly fabulous, especially if just seared but not frazzled. Remember to thaw them completely before you cook them and dry them well too.

griddled king scallops
with chilli, lime and spring onions

SERVES 4

2.5 ml/½ tsp chilli powder
5 ml/1 tsp paprika
Finely grated zest and juice of 1 lime
Salt and freshly ground black pepper
24 king scallops, thawed if frozen
60 ml/4 tbsp olive oil
2 bunches of spring onions
 (scallions), trimmed but left whole

A few fresh coriander (cilantro) or
 flatleaf parsley leaves and
 wedges of lime, for garnishing

TO SERVE:
Olive ciabatta bread

1 Mix together the chilli, paprika, lime zest and juice and a light seasoning of salt and pepper. Toss with the scallops, then add 15 ml/1 tbsp of the oil and toss again. Leave to marinate for up to 30 minutes.

2 Preheat the grill.

3 Toss the spring onions in 15 ml/1 tbsp of the remaining oil. Lay them on the grill, close the lid and cook 2 minutes. Remove and keep warm.

4 Reheat the grill. Drain the scallops well, place them on the grill, close the lid and cook for 1 minute only.

5 Transfer the scallops and springs onions to warm plates. Drizzle the remaining olive oil around, garnish with a few coriander or parsley leaves and wedges of lime.

6 Serve with olive ciabatta bread.

If your fish are large, you may have to cook them two at a time and keep the first ones warm in a low oven while you cook the remainder. The cool but spicy salsa offsets the richness of this often-neglected but fabulous fish.

sizzling mackerel with fresh tomato chilli salsa

SERVES 4

FOR THE SALSA:
4 tomatoes, skinned, seeded and finely chopped
2 spring onions (scallions), finely chopped
1 red chilli, seeded and finely chopped
15 ml/1 tbsp chopped fresh parsley
15 ml/1 tbsp chopped fresh coriander (cilantro)
10 ml/2 tsp clear honey
Grated zest and juice of 1 lime
Salt and freshly ground black pepper

FOR THE FISH:
4 mackerel, cleaned and heads removed
4 bay leaves
15 ml/1 tbsp olive oil
Wedges of lime, for garnishing

TO SERVE:
Plain potatoes or flour tortillas

1 Put all the salsa ingredients in a bowl with just a little salt and pepper and mix well. Leave to stand until ready to serve.

2 Rinse the fish under cold running water. Pat dry on kitchen paper (paper towels). Push a bay leaf inside the cavity of each fish. Make several slashes in the flesh on each side. Season lightly.

3 Preheat the grill. Brush the fish with a little olive oil on each side. Place the fish on the grill, close the lid and cook for 4 minutes until griddle-browned and cooked through.

4 Transfer to warm plates and garnish with wedges of lime.

5 Serve with the salsa and plain potatoes or flour tortillas.

Smoked mackerel is often served cold with a dollop of horseradish relish, but here it is griddled with a hint of onion, then served with a light, fluffy but creamy mousse, well-flavoured with horseradish for a much more exciting experience.

hot smoked mackerel
with horseradish mousse

SERVES 4

4 large smoked mackerel fillets
A little sunflower oil
1 small onion, finely chopped

FOR THE MOUSSE:
90 ml/6 tbsp double (heavy) cream
30 ml/2 tbsp horseradish relish

1 egg white
Freshly ground black pepper
Sprigs of fresh parsley and wedges
   of lemon, for garnishing

TO SERVE:
New potatoes and a green salad

1 Brush the mackerel with oil and sprinkle with the chopped onion.

2 Make the mousse. Whip the cream until peaking. Fold the horseradish into the cream.

3 Whisk the egg white until stiff, then fold into the horseradish cream with a metal spoon. Chill until ready to serve. Meanwhile, preheat the grill.

4 Lay the fish on the grill. Close the lid and cook for 2 minutes only. Transfer to warm plates and garnish with sprigs of fresh parsley and wedges of lemon.

5 Serve with the horseradish mousse, new potatoes and a green salad.

The bigger the prawns, the better the result will be. Thaw them completely if frozen, then dry them well and, most importantly, leave their shells on! Throw them on the grill as if it were a barbecue, then close the lid so they cook very, very quickly.

griddled king prawns with aioli

SERVES 4

150 ml/¹/₄ pt/²/₃ cup mayonnaise
2 garlic cloves, crushed
24 raw unshelled king prawns
 (jumbo shrimp), thawed if frozen

Wedges of lemon and a little
 chopped fresh parsley, for
 garnishing

TO SERVE:
French bread

1 To make the aioli, mix the mayonnaise with the garlic, then cover and chill until ready to serve.

2 Preheat the grill. Dry the prawns on kitchen paper (paper towels).

3 Lay the prawns on the grill. Close the lid and cook for 2 minutes until pink throughout and slightly charred in places.

4 Place on warm plates and garnish with wedges of lemon and a little chopped parsley.

5 Serve with French bread and the aioli on the side.

Red mullet is an exciting fish, often overlooked for other more familiar types. Here it is simply griddled with a fragrant herb butter to make a delicious dish – nothing could be more fresh or succulent.

red mullet with parsley butter

SERVES 4

4 red mullet, cleaned
Finely grated zest and juice of
  1 small lemon
A little sunflower oil
50 g/2 oz/¼ cup softened butter

Freshly ground black pepper
45 ml/3 tbsp chopped fresh parsley

TO SERVE:
Sauté potatoes and peas

1 Scrape all the scales off the fish. Rinse and pat dry on kitchen paper (paper towels). Sprinkle all over with the lemon juice, then brush with about 30 ml/2 tbsp of the oil.

2 Mash the butter with a good grinding of pepper, the lemon zest and parsley. Shape into a short roll on greaseproof (waxed) paper, wrap and chill.

3 Oil the grill, then preheat it. Lay the fish on the grill. Close the lid and cook for 4–5 minutes until cooked through.

4 Transfer to warm plates. Cut the parsley butter into four or eight slices and put them on the fish.

5 Serve straight away with sauté potatoes and peas.

Tuna steaks cook quickly and perfectly on your health grill. Don't be tempted to cook them too long, however – they should still be pink in the centre. Serve them with a smooth, cool avocado dip for a delicious, light, but satisfying meal.

fresh tuna with guacamole salsa

SERVES 4

1 onion, thinly sliced
1 garlic clove, crushed
1 green chilli, seeded and chopped
30 ml/2 tbsp olive oil
5 ml/1 tsp lemon juice
Salt and freshly ground black pepper
4 fresh tuna steaks

FOR THE SALSA:
2 ripe avocados, halved and stoned
   (pitted)
15 ml/1 tbsp lemon juice
5 ml/1 tsp grated onion

150 ml/¼ pt/⅔ cup olive oil
Tabasco sauce
Worcestershire sauce
1 small green (bell) pepper, finely
   chopped
1 small red pepper, finely chopped
A little sunflower oil
Sprigs of fresh parsley, for
   garnishing

TO SERVE:
Warm flour tortillas, black olives and
   a green salad

1 Mix the onion, garlic, chilli, olive oil and lemon juice with a little salt and pepper in a shallow dish. Add the tuna, turn to coat and leave to marinate for 2 hours.

2 Meanwhile, make the salsa. Scoop the avocado flesh into a bowl and mash with the lemon juice. Add the onion, then gradually beat in the oil to form a smooth, thick salsa. Add a dash each of Tabasco and Worcestershire sauce and season to taste. Stir in the peppers, then spoon into a bowl.

3 Oil the grill, then preheat it. Drain the tuna steaks well and lay them on the grill. Close the lid and grill for 3 minutes only until still slightly pink in the centre.

4 Transfer to warm plates and garnish with sprigs of fresh parsley.

5 Serve with the guacamole salsa, flour tortillas, black olives and a green salad.

These swordfish steaks are seasoned with coconut, lemon grass, chilli and coriander. All you have to do is griddle them and serve them on sticky fragrant rice for a truly exotic, typically Thai experience.

thai-style swordfish steaks with sticky rice

SERVES 4

4 swordfish steaks
1 x 400 g/14 oz/large can of
   coconut milk
Sunflower oil
2 garlic cloves, crushed
5 ml/1 tsp crushed lemon grass
5 ml/1 tsp Thai fish sauce
1 small green chilli, seeded and
   chopped

15 ml/1 tbsp chopped fresh
   coriander (cilantro)
Grated zest and juice of 1 lime
225 g/8 oz/1 cup Thai fragrant rice
Salt
Wedges of lime and a few fresh
   coriander leaves, for garnishing

TO SERVE:
A mixed salad

1 Wipe the fish and place in a single layer in a large, shallow dish.

2 Mix together 45 ml/3 tbsp of the coconut milk, 45 ml/3 tbsp of the sunflower oil and all the remaining ingredients, except the rice and salt, and pour over the fish. Turn to coat completely, then leave to marinate for at least 2 hours, turning once.

3 Drain off the marinade into a saucepan. Add the remaining coconut milk and bring to the boil. Boil rapidly until reduced by half, stirring occasionally. Season to taste. Keep warm.

4 Cook the rice in plenty of boiling, lightly salted water according to the packet directions. Drain.

5 Meanwhile, oil the grill, then preheat it. Drain the fish steaks well and lay them on the grill, close the lid and cook for 4 minutes until just cooked through.

6 Spoon the cooked Thai rice into shallow bowls. Top with the fish, then pour the sauce over and garnish with wedges of lime and a few coriander leaves.

7 Serve with a mixed salad.

Even people who say they hate raw oysters will simply melt when they try these! The oysters are opened and immediately griddled until sizzling in their juices, then laced with cream and freshly grated Parmesan. Cook in two batches, if necessary.

grilled oysters
with cream and parmesan

SERVES 4

16 oysters in their shells	90 ml/6 tbsp double (heavy) cream
Freshly ground black pepper	90 ml/6 tbsp freshly grated
A few drops of Tabasco sauce	Parmesan cheese

1 Preheat the grill. Shuck (open) the oysters: hold each one firmly in an oven-gloved hand, insert the point of a knife near the hinge, then twist until the oyster opens. Take care not to spill the juice.

2 Place the half shells containing the oysters and their juices on the grill. Season each with a grinding of pepper and a dash of Tabasco sauce. Cook on the open grill until the juices start to sizzle.

3 Spoon over the cream and top with a little Parmesan. Holding the lid, lower it until it is just above the oysters and cook for 1 minute until the cream and cheese are just bubbling.

4 Remove the oysters carefully so you don't damage the grill plates. Serve straight away.

Crab cakes are just so good, they have to be included here. They are much better griddled than fried – it brings out the full flavour of the seafood and the other ingredients so they can be fully appreciated.

crab and pimiento cakes with orange mayonnaise

SERVES 4

120 ml/4 fl oz/½ cup mayonnaise
Finely grated zest and juice
  of 1 orange
2 x 170 g/6 oz/small cans of white
  crabmeat, drained
100 g/4 oz/2 cups fresh white
  breadcrumbs
1 x 200 g/7 oz/small can of
  pimientos, drained and chopped
30 ml/2 tbsp snipped fresh chives

15 ml/1 tbsp chopped fresh
  coriander (cilantro)
1.5 ml/¼ tsp cayenne
Salt and freshly ground black pepper
A little milk, if necessary
5 ml/1 tsp lemon juice
45 ml/3 tbsp crème fraîche
A little sunflower oil

TO SERVE:
A mixed salad

1   Put 90 ml/6 tbsp of the mayonnaise in a bowl with half the orange juice. Add the crabmeat, half the breadcrumbs, all the pimientos and the herbs.

2   Mix thoroughly and season to taste with the cayenne, salt and pepper. Moisten with a little milk, if necessary.

3   Shape into eight small cakes and coat in the remaining breadcrumbs. Chill until ready to cook.

4   Mix the remaining mayonnaise with the zest and remaining juice of the orange, the lemon juice, crème fraîche and seasoning to taste. Chill.

5   Preheat the grill. Brush the crab cakes with oil. Place on the grill. If you have an adjustable grill, lower the lid so it sits gently on the cakes and cook for about 4 minutes until griddle-browned and cooked through. If not, cook on the open grill for 4 minutes on each side.

6   Serve with the chilled orange mayonnaise and a mixed salad.

Monkfish is the most succulent and robust of fish. Here, small thick steaks are flavoured with smoky pimentón, seared to perfection and served with a delicious salad of rice, peas, toasted pine nuts and sweet raisins.

monkfish medallions with pimentón and toasted pine nut and rice salad

SERVES 4

4 monkfish medallions,
    about 150 g/5 oz each
15 ml/1 tbsp pimentón
60 ml/4 tbsp olive oil
30 ml/2 tbsp lemon juice
100 g/4 oz/¹/₂ cup long-grain rice
50 g/2 oz/¹/₂ cup frozen peas

50 g/2 oz/¹/₂ cup pine nuts
50 g/2 oz/¹/₃ cup raisins
5 ml/1 tsp Dijon mustard
5 ml/1 tsp caster (superfine) sugar
Salt and freshly ground black pepper
A few salad leaves, for garnishing

1 Wipe the fish with kitchen paper (paper towels).

2 Mix the pimentón with half the oil and half the lemon juice. Brush all over the fish and leave to marinate for 2 hours.

3 Cook the rice in boiling, lightly salted water for 10 minutes until just tender but still with some 'bite', adding the peas after 5 minutes' cooking time. Drain, rinse with cold water and drain again.

4 Dry-fry the pine nuts in a frying pan until turning golden. Tip out of the pan straight away. Add to the rice with the raisins.

5 Preheat the grill. Place the fish on the grill. If you have an adjustable grill, lower the lid so it sits gently on the fish and cook for 3–4 minutes until just cooked through. If not, cook on the open grill for 3–4 minutes on each side, pressing down lightly with a spatula.

6 Meanwhile, whisk the remaining oil with the remaining lemon juice, the mustard, sugar and a little salt and pepper. Pour over the rice salad and toss well.

7 Spoon the rice salad on to plates. Add a swordfish steak to each plate, garnish with a few salad leaves and serve.

Trout is traditionally served with almonds but here the tradition is extended to include garlic, fresh parsley and olive oil. They all enhance the fish perfectly. If your trout are large, you may have to cook them two at a time. If so, keep the first ones warm.

trout with parsley and almond pesto

SERVES 4

4 trout, cleaned and heads removed

FOR THE PESTO:
1 large garlic clove, halved
50 g/2 oz/¹/₂ cup ground almonds
A handful of fresh parsley
90 ml/6 tbsp olive oil, plus a little for brushing
30 ml/2 tbsp freshly grated Parmesan cheese

A good squeeze of lemon juice
Salt and freshly ground black pepper
Wedges of lemon and sprigs of fresh parsley, for garnishing

TO SERVE:
New potatoes and French (green) beans

1   Rinse the trout under cold running water and pat dry on kitchen paper (paper towels).

2   Make the pesto. Put the garlic, almonds and parsley in a blender or food processor. Run the machine to blend, then, with the machine still running, add the oil in a thin stream, stopping and scraping down the sides occasionally until a thick paste is formed. Blend in the Parmesan, sharpen with lemon juice and season to taste.

3   Spoon the mixture into the cavities of the fish. Brush the outer surfaces with a little olive oil.

4   Oil, then preheat the grill. Lay the fish on the grill, close the lid and cook for 4 minutes. Transfer to warm plates and garnish with wedges of lemon and sprigs of fresh parsley.

5   Serve with new potatoes and French beans.

VEGETARIAN
GRILLS

You don't have to be a vegetarian to want to try the dishes in this section. Everyone will enjoy the pleasures of glorious vegetables griddled to perfection and served in a variety of sumptuous sauces, dips and dressings. All these recipes have enough protein to make them highly nutritious main courses and should tempt even the most avid meat-eater to try them.

This is delicious on its own or as an accompaniment to plain grilled meat or even Quorn steaks. I often make twice the amount of fondue, just so I can keep dipping my French bread into it!

griddled courgettes and aubergines with fondue dip

SERVES 4

2 small aubergines (eggplants)
2 large courgettes (zucchini)
45 ml/3 tbsp olive oil
1 garlic clove, chopped
5 ml/1 tsp Italian seasoning
Coarse sea salt, for garnishing

FOR THE FONDUE:
100 g/4 oz/1 cup grated Cheddar
  cheese

100 g/4 oz/1 cup grated Gruyère
  (Swiss) cheese
15 ml/1 tbsp cornflour (cornstarch)
150 ml/¼ pt/⅔ cup milk
150 ml/¼ pt/⅔ cup crème fraîche
30 ml/2 tbsp vodka or kirsch
Salt and freshly ground black pepper

TO SERVE:
French bread and a large mixed
  salad

1 Cut the vegetables diagonally into fairly thick slices. Toss in the oil with the garlic and seasoning and leave until ready to cook.

2 Mix all the fondue ingredients except the salt and pepper together in a saucepan and heat gently, stirring all the time, until bubbling, thick and smooth. Season to taste.

3 Preheat the grill. Lay the vegetables on the grill. Close the lid and cook for 6–8 minutes or until tender. Cook in two batches, if necessary.

4 Meanwhile, reheat the fondue and spoon into four small warm bowls.

5 Transfer the vegetables to warm plates and sprinkle with coarse sea salt. Put a pot of fondue on each plate.

6 Serve with lots of crusty bread and round the meal off with a large mixed salad.

The coconut dip adds richness and depth to the kebabs, which are a delicious mix of sweet and savoury flavours. Try them with peanut or cashew nut sauce too, for a mouth-watering change (see page 86).

vegetable and fruit kebabs with spicy coconut dip

SERVES 4

1 sweetcorn (corn) cob, cut into 8 chunks
1 large courgette (zucchini), cut into 8 chunks
1 large under-ripe banana, peeled and cut into 8 chunks
8 tomatoes
30 ml/2 tbsp olive oil
5 ml/1 tsp lemon juice
Salt and freshly ground black pepper

FOR THE DIP:
90 ml/6 tbsp white wine vinegar
90 ml/6 tbsp water

30 ml/2 tbsp clear honey
1/2 x 250g/9 oz block of creamed coconut
1 green chilli, seeded and chopped
5 ml/1 tsp grated fresh root ginger
30 ml/2 tbsp soy sauce
15 ml/1 tbsp chopped fresh coriander (cilantro)
A little sunflower oil
Sprigs of fresh coriander, for garnishing

TO SERVE:
Rice and a green salad

1 Thread a piece of each vegetable and fruit on to eight wooden skewers that have been soaked in cold water. Brush with half the oil and the lemon juice and season lightly.

2 To make the dip, boil the vinegar, water and honey for 3 minutes, stirring, until the liquid is reduced. Stir in the coconut until dissolved. Stir in the remaining ingredients and add the remaining olive oil. Keep warm.

3 Oil the grill, then preheat it. Lay the kebabs on the grill. If you have an adjustable grill, lower the lid so it rests lightly on top of the kebabs and cook for 6 minutes. If not, cook on the open grill for 6 minutes on each side until griddle-browned and tender.

4 Transfer to warm plates and garnish with sprigs of coriander.

5 Serve on a bed of rice with the warm coconut dip and a green salad.

Rustic-style patties, griddled until golden and still moist inside, and served with a creamy, spicy sauce. If you're in a hurry, you could buy a jar of ready-made korma sauce and simply heat it in a saucepan.

lentil and mushroom patties with curry sauce

SERVES 4

FOR THE PATTIES:
225 g/8 oz/1¹/₃ cups brown lentils, soaked for several hours in cold water
1 onion, finely chopped
1 garlic clove, crushed
100 g/4 oz mushrooms, finely chopped
60 ml/4 tbsp sunflower oil, plus extra for brushing
2.5 ml/¹/₂ tsp chilli powder
5 ml/1 tsp garam masala
30 ml/2 tbsp smooth mango chutney
75 g/3 oz/1¹/₂ cups fresh breadcrumbs
30 ml/2 tbsp chopped fresh coriander (cilantro)

1 egg, beaten
Salt and freshly ground black pepper

FOR THE SAUCE:
1 onion, finely chopped
1 garlic clove, crushed
A little sunflower oil
45 ml/3 tbsp mild curry paste
50 g/2 oz/¹/₃ cup raisins
1 x 400 g/14 oz/large can of coconut milk
Wedges of lemon and sprigs of fresh coriander, for garnishing

TO SERVE:
Rice and a side salad

1   Drain the lentils, place in a saucepan and add just enough water to cover. Bring to the boil and boil rapidly for 10 minutes, then reduce the heat and simmer for about 1 hour or until the lentils are tender and have absorbed all the liquid.

2   Meanwhile, fry (sauté) the onion, garlic and mushrooms in the oil for 2 minutes, stirring. Stir in the spices and cook for a further 30 seconds, then remove from the heat. Stir in the lentils and the remaining patty ingredients, seasoning to taste with salt and pepper. Leave until cool enough to handle then shape into eight flat cakes. Chill until ready to cook.

3 Make the sauce. Fry the onion and garlic in 15 ml/1 tbsp of the sunflower oil for 1 minute, stirring. Stir in the curry paste and fry for a further minute, stirring. Stir in the raisins and coconut milk. Bring to the boil, stirring, reduce the heat and simmer for 10 minutes until slightly thickened. Season to taste.

4 Oil the grill, then preheat it. Brush the cakes with oil, then place on the grill. If you have an adjustable grill, lower the lid so it rests lightly on top of the patties and cook for 4–5 minutes until griddle-browned and cooked through. If not, cook on the open grill for 4–5 minutes on each side, pressing down lightly with a spatula.

5 Transfer to warm plates and garnish with wedges of lemon and sprigs of coriander.

6 Serve with the sauce, rice and a side salad.

*This delicious array of griddled vegetables is truly fabulous!
Make sure you have plenty of warm Italian bread to serve with
it and follow it with a crisp, cool salad. Then, if you're still
hungry, I would suggest a platter of Italian cheeses.*

grilled italian platter

SERVES 4

1 fennel bulb, cut lengthways into
    5 mm/¹/₄ in slices
2 small courgettes (zucchini), cut
    lengthways into 5 mm/¹/₄ in slices
1 small aubergine (eggplant), cut
    lengthways into 5 mm/¹/₄ in slices
2 onions, quartered
1 red (bell) pepper, quartered
1 x 400 g/14 oz/large can of
    artichoke hearts, drained
4 large open mushrooms, peeled

FOR THE MARINADE:
60 ml/4 tbsp olive oil
1 garlic clove, crushed
Grated zest and juice of 1 lime
Salt and freshly ground black pepper

TO FINISH:
100 g/4 oz/1 cup grated Mozzarella
    cheese
30 ml/2 tbsp sliced black olives
A few fresh basil leaves, torn

TO SERVE:
Ciabatta bread

1 Cook the fennel in boiling, lightly salted water for 3 minutes.
Drain, rinse with cold water and drain again.

2 Put all the prepared vegetables in a large, shallow dish.

3 Mix the marinade ingredients together and drizzle over the
vegetables. Toss gently.

4 Preheat the grill. Lift the vegetables out of the marinade with a
draining spoon and place as many as you can fit on the grill, close
the lid and cook for 5 minutes. Remove and keep warm. Reheat
the grill and cook the remaining vegetables in the same way.

5 Transfer the vegetables to warm plates and sprinkle with the
grated cheese, olives and torn basil leaves.

6 Serve with ciabatta bread.

These lightly spiced cakes can be made plain without the corn as an accompaniment to other dishes. You can use scooped-out potato from the potato nests on page 24 or cook two medium potatoes in the microwave, then scoop out the flesh.

potato and corn cakes with cumin

SERVES 4

About 225 g/8 oz/1 cup cooked
  potato
1 x 200 g/7 oz/small can of
  sweetcorn (corn), drained
1 small onion, grated
1 small green chilli, seeded and
  chopped

2.5 ml/½ tsp ground cumin
10 ml/2 tsp plain (all-purpose) flour
Salt and freshly ground black pepper
1 egg, beaten
A little sunflower oil

TO SERVE:
Mango chutney and a mixed salad

1 Mix everything except the egg and oil together until well blended.

2 Stir in the beaten egg to bind.

3 Shape into eight or 12 small cakes and flatten slightly. Chill for at least 30 minutes.

4 Oil the grill and preheat it.

5 Place the cakes on the grill. Close the lid and cook for 3–4 minutes until griddle-browned and fairly crisp on the outside. Transfer to warm plates.

6 Serve with mango chutney and a mixed salad.

This classic Mediterranean combination makes a delicious starter to serve before a pasta dish, or a light lunch served with a salad and crusty bread. You could even use the mixture as a hot filling for crusty baguettes or ciabatta rolls.

griddled aubergine
with tomato, basil and mozzarella

SERVES 4

1 large aubergine (eggplant)
A little olive oil
60 ml/4 tbsp tomato purée (paste)
5 ml/1 tsp dried basil
Salt and freshly ground black pepper

175 g/6 oz Mozzarella cheese,
   sliced
A few fresh basil leaves, torn

TO SERVE:
Warm focaccia bread

1   Preheat the grill. Trim the ends off the aubergine and slice lengthways into four thick slices.

2   Brush the slices with olive oil on both sides.

3   Place on the grill, close the lid and cook for 3 minutes.

4   Open the lid, loosen the slices. Spread with the tomato purée, then sprinkle with dried basil and a little salt and pepper. Top with slices of cheese. Holding the lid, lower it until it is just above the cheese and continue to cook for about 30 seconds until the cheese is melting.

5   Transfer to warm plates, drizzle with a little more olive oil and sprinkle with the torn fresh basil leaves.

6   Serve with warm focaccia bread.

Cauliflower and cheese have always been firm favourites and here is a way of getting those delicious tastes combined in a griddled cake. If you don't have time to prepare the sauce and other accompaniments, serve it with canned plum tomatoes.

cauliflower cheese griddle with fresh tomato sauce

SERVES 4

1 small cauliflower, separated into small florets
100 g/4 oz/1 cup grated mature Cheddar cheese
5 ml/1 tsp made English mustard
50 g/2 oz/1 cup fresh white breadcrumbs
Salt and freshly ground black pepper
2 eggs, beaten

FOR THE FRESH TOMATO SAUCE:
1 bunch of spring onions (scallions), finely chopped

Sunflower oil
3 beefsteak tomatoes, skinned and chopped
15 ml/1 tbsp tomato purée (paste)
5 ml/1 tsp caster (superfine) sugar
2.5 ml/¹/₂ tsp dried mixed herbs
Sprigs of fresh parsley, for garnishing

TO SERVE:
Baby new potatoes and peas

1 Cook the cauliflower in boiling, salted water for about 5 minutes or until tender. Drain thoroughly and leave until cold.

2 Mash the cold cauliflower with a potato masher, then stir in the cheese, mustard, breadcrumbs and a little salt and pepper. Mix with the beaten eggs to bind.

3 Make the sauce. Fry the spring onions in 15 ml/1 tbsp of the oil for 2 minutes, stirring. Add the remaining ingredients and simmer, stirring, for about 5 minutes or until pulpy. Season to taste.

4 Liberally oil the grill, then preheat it. Spread the cauliflower mixture out over the whole area of the grill. Close the lid and cook for 4 minutes until lightly golden and set. Divide into quarters. Transfer to warm plates and garnish with parsley.

5 Serve with the fresh tomato sauce, baby new potatoes and peas.

These tasty morsels are usually deep-fried but here they become a mouth-watering low-fat phenomenon. They are equally delicious with the minted fromage frais dressing on page 31 or the spiced yoghurt on page 50.

grilled falafels
with cucumber and dill dressing

SERVES 4

FOR THE FALAFELS:
1 x 425 g/15 oz/large can of chick
   peas (garbanzos), drained
1 red onion, quartered
1 garlic clove, crushed
2.5 ml/¹/₂ tsp chilli powder
5 ml/1 tsp ground cumin
5 ml/1 tsp caraway seeds
1 large sprig of fresh parsley
30 ml/2 tbsp plain (all-purpose) flour
Salt and freshly ground black pepper
1 egg, beaten

75 g/3 oz/³/₄ cup dried breadcrumbs

FOR THE DRESSING:
5 cm/2 in piece of cucumber, grated
1 small garlic clove, crushed
10 ml/2 tsp dried dill (dill weed)
150 ml/¹/₄ pt/²/₃ cup thick plain
   yoghurt
A little sunflower oil

TO SERVE:
Warm pitta breads and salad

1   Put all the falafel ingredients except the egg and breadcrumbs in a food processor and run the machine until the mixture forms a paste, stopping and scraping down the sides as necessary.

2   Shape the mixture into 12 small balls. Roll them in the egg, then the breadcrumbs, to coat completely.

3   Make the dressing. Squeeze the grated cucumber to remove excess liquid. Mix with the garlic, dill and yoghurt and season lightly. Chill until ready to serve.

4   Oil and preheat the grill. Place half the cakes on the grill. Close the lid and cook for 6 minutes. Keep these warm while you cook the remainder.

5   Serve with the yoghurt dressing, warm pitta breads and salad.

These sensational kebabs are bathed in a sharp, fruity passion fruit dressing. I find it best to cook the denser vegetables a little first so they all griddle to the same consistency – otherwise you'll have overcooked tomatoes and still-crunchy courgettes!

vegetable and tofu kebabs with passion fruit dressing

SERVES 4

16 baby new potatoes
1 leek, cut into 8 pieces
1 courgette (zucchini), cut into
    8 pieces
8 button mushrooms
8 cherry tomatoes
1 x 250 g/9 oz block of plain or
    smoked tofu, cubed
75 ml/5 tbsp olive oil

FOR THE DRESSING:
1 passion fruit
15 ml/1 tbsp lemon juice
10 ml/2 tsp clear honey
Salt and freshly ground black pepper

TO SERVE:
Crusty bread and a mixed salad

1 Cook the potatoes in boiling, lightly salted water for 3 minutes, then add the leek and courgette and cook for a further 3 minutes until almost tender.

2 Preheat the grill. Thread the cooked vegetables, mushrooms, tomatoes and tofu on to eight wooden skewers that have been soaked in cold water. Brush with some of the oil.

3 Place the kebabs on the grill and close the lid. Grill for about 3 minutes until cooked and golden.

4 Meanwhile, halve the passion fruit and scoop the seeds into a small saucepan. Whisk in the remaining oil with the remaining dressing ingredients and heat through.

5 Place the kebabs on warm plates and drizzle the dressing over.

6 Serve straight away with crusty bread and a mixed salad.

If you can't find cashew nut butter, you can purée the nuts yourself in a blender or food processor, adding 15–30 ml/ 1–2 tbsp sunflower oil to form a thick, smooth paste. You can also use peanut butter if you prefer.

sweet potato sticks and baby corn cobs with cashew and chilli sauce

SERVES 4

2 sweet potatoes, peeled and cut
  into thick sticks
250 g/9 oz baby corn cobs
2.5 ml/½ tsp chilli powder
60 ml/4 tbsp olive oil
5 ml/1 tsp dried oregano

FOR THE SAUCE:
100 g/4 oz/½ cup cashew nut butter
1 green chilli, seeded and finely
  chopped

250 ml/8 fl oz/1 cup vegetable
  stock, made with 1 stock cube
10 ml/2 tsp soy sauce
60 ml/4 tbsp milk
15 ml/1 tbsp chopped fresh parsley,
  for garnishing

TO SERVE:
Wholegrain bread and a large mixed
  salad

1 Put the sweet potato sticks and corn cobs in separate bowls. Add the chilli powder and half the olive oil to the sweet potato and toss with your hands to coat completely. Add the remaining olive oil and the oregano to the corn cobs and toss.

2 Preheat the grill. Lay the sweet potato sticks on the grill. Close the lid and cook for 12 minutes or until griddle-browned and cooked through. Remove from the grill and keep warm.

3 Reheat the grill, add the corn, close the lid and cook for 5 minutes.

4 Meanwhile, put all the sauce ingredients except the milk in a saucepan and stir well. Bring to the boil, stirring, until smooth. Thin with the milk.

5 Transfer the sweet potato sticks and corn cobs to warm plates and scatter the parsley over.

6 Serve with the cashew sauce, wholegrain bread and a large mixed salad.

Slabs of yellow polenta, coated in crunchy couscous and tasty Parmesan and griddled until golden, served with juicy tomatoes, filled with fragrant pesto and melting Mozzarella. You can make your own polenta slab, but this is much quicker!

grilled golden polenta with italian tomatoes

SERVES 4

2 beefsteak tomatoes
Salt and freshly ground black pepper
30 ml/2 tbsp pesto
50 g/2 oz/½ cup grated Mozzarella cheese
1 slab of ready-made polenta
45 ml/3 tbsp plain (all-purpose) flour
40 g/1½ oz/¼ cup couscous

25 g/1 oz/¼ cup freshly grated Parmesan cheese
1 egg, beaten
A little olive oil
Sprigs of fresh basil, for garnishing

TO SERVE:
Olive ciabatta bread and a green salad

1   Halve the tomatoes, scoop out the seeds and discard. Season the insides with pepper.

2   Divide the pesto among the tomatoes, then fill with the Mozzarella cheese.

3   Cut the polenta into eight thick slices and pat dry on kitchen paper (paper towels). Season the flour with a little salt and pepper. Mix the couscous with the Parmesan. Dip the polenta in the seasoned flour, then the egg, then the couscous mixture, to coat completely.

4   Oil the grill, then preheat it. Place the polenta on the grill. Close the lid and cook for about 4 minutes until golden. Remove from the grill and keep warm.

5   Wipe down the grill, then reheat it. Put the tomatoes on the grill. Close the lid and cook for 1 minute only, to melt the cheese. The tomatoes should still be holding their shape.

6   Transfer to warm plates with the polenta and garnish with sprigs of basil.

7   Serve with olive ciabatta bread and a green salad.

These tasty burgers are also good topped with a slice of cheese after cooking but while still on the grill. Hold the lid over the cheese, not quite touching, for about 30 seconds until the cheese is melting.

griddle-style veggie burgers

SERVES 4

A little sunflower oil
1 small onion, finely chopped
1 red (bell) pepper, finely chopped
1 x 300 g/11 oz/medium can of petit pois with carrots, thoroughly drained
100 g/4 oz/1 cup cooked long-grain rice

5 ml/1 tsp dried mixed herbs
Salt and freshly ground black pepper
90 ml/6 tbsp plain (all-purpose) flour
1 egg, beaten

TO SERVE:
Large burger buns, mayonnaise and a large salad

1   Heat 15 ml/1 tbsp of the oil in a saucepan, add the onion and pepper and fry, stirring, for 3 minutes until softened and lightly golden. Remove from the heat.

2   Add the peas and carrots and mash with a potato masher. Stir in the rice, herbs, a little salt and pepper, the flour and the beaten egg.

3   Oil the grill, then preheat it. Shape the mixture into four cakes and place on the grill. Close the lid and cook for 5 minutes.

4   Transfer to large burger buns, top each with a dollop of mayonnaise and serve with a large salad.

Quorn is so versatile it can take on almost any flavour. Here it is cooked with a simple barbecue sauce to make it slightly sticky and rich. The trick is to grill it long enough to give it a glorious glaze but not so long that it burns. Check often during cooking.

barbecued quorn steaks

SERVES 4

15 ml/1 tbsp golden (light corn)
  syrup
30 ml/2 tbsp tomato purée (paste)
10 ml/2 tsp Worcestershire sauce
10 ml/2 tsp soy sauce
15 ml/1 tbsp red wine vinegar
1.5 ml/¼ tsp pimentón
Freshly ground black pepper
4 Quorn steaks

A little sunflower or olive oil
100 g/4 oz/2 cups beansprouts
1 small green (bell) pepper, very
  thinly sliced
1 small red pepper, very thinly sliced

TO SERVE:
Tagliatelle tossed in olive oil with
  a handful of toasted pine nuts

1 Mix together the syrup, tomato purée, Worcestershire and soy sauces, vinegar, pimentón and a little pepper in a shallow dish.

2 Add the Quorn steaks and turn to coat with the mixture. Leave to marinate for at least 2 hours, turning once or twice.

3 Oil the grill, then preheat it. Drain the Quorn, place on the grill, close the lid and cook for 3–4 minutes, opening and brushing with any remaining marinade once during cooking.

4 Mix the beansprouts and peppers together. Transfer the steaks to warm plates and garnish with the beansprout mixture.

5 Serve with tagliatelle tossed in olive oil with toasted pine nuts.

Highly nutritious and delicious 'sandwiches' with not a slice of bread in sight! Slices of aubergine are filled with a gorgeous, nutty cake, and griddled until golden. They are then bathed in a simple but delicious tomato sauce.

cracked wheat patty and aubergine sandwiches

SERVES 4

1 litre/1³/₄ pts/4¹/₄ cups water
100 g/4 oz/1 cup cornmeal
15 ml/1 tbsp peanut butter
Salt and freshly ground black pepper
75 g/3 oz/³/₄ cup salted peanuts, finely chopped
175 g/6 oz/1 cup bulgar (cracked wheat)
2 small aubergines (eggplants)
1 garlic clove, crushed

30 ml/2 tbsp chopped fresh parsley
A good pinch of cayenne
A little olive oil
200 ml/7 fl oz/scant 1 cup passata (sieved tomatoes)
2.5 ml/¹/₂ tsp dried oregano
10 ml/2 tsp clear honey

TO SERVE:
Rocket salad

1   Bring 500 ml/17 fl oz/2¹/₄ cups of the water to the boil in a large pan. Add the cornmeal, peanut butter and a little pepper. Cook over a very gentle heat, stirring frequently, for about 3 minutes until the mixture is very thick and leaves the sides of the pan clean. Stir in the peanuts and leave to cool.

2   Put the bulgar in a heavy pan and cook gently for about 4 minutes until lightly toasted, stirring as it heats. Add the remaining water and bring to the boil, then cover the pan, reduce the heat and simmer for about 20 minutes, stirring occasionally to prevent sticking. Season with salt and pepper.

3   Cut the stalks off the aubergines, then cut each lengthways into four thick slices.

4   Work the cornmeal and bulgar mixtures together with your hands, adding the garlic, parsley and cayenne. Shape into four oval, flat patties, just smaller than the aubergine slices. Chill well.

5 Preheat the grill. Brush the patties with oil and place on the grill. Close the lid and cook for 5 minutes until the patties are griddle-browned. Remove and keep warm.

6 Brush the aubergine slices with oil. Place on the grill, close the lid and cook for 5 minutes or until griddle-browned and tender but not soggy. Cook in two batches if necessary.

7 Meanwhile, mix the passata with the oregano and honey in a small saucepan and season lightly. Heat through.

8 Transfer one of the aubergine slices to each of four plates and top with a patty, then another aubergine slice. Spoon a little warm passata sauce over each sandwich.

9 Serve with a rocket salad.

TOASTED SANDWICHES
AND OTHER BREAD SNACKS

Well, you can say goodbye to your toasted sandwich maker. Now you can make an amazing variety of mouth-watering snacks, ranging from good old toasted sandwiches to panini and calzones (like closed pizza pies). They will all have that lovely griddled look and can be cooked in just a few minutes.

There's a classic combination of sliced meat, cheese and fruit in this delicious toasted creation. Ring the changes with chorizo or pepperoni instead of salami, and blue cheese, like Dolcelatte, or a creamy one, like Port Salut, instead of Cheddar.

cheese, salami and tomato panini

MAKES 2

A little sunflower oil
2 small part-baked baguettes
10 ml/2 tsp Dijon mustard
8 slices of salami

2 tomatoes, sliced
50 g/2 oz/½ cup grated Cheddar
  cheese

1 Oil the grill and preheat it, then turn it down to the lowest setting.

2 Split the baguettes and open out slightly. Spread with the mustard.

3 Fill with the salami, tomatoes and cheese.

4 Place on the grill. Close and cook for 4 minutes until griddle-browned on the outside and the cheese has melted.

Use the rest of this sauce for dinner with spaghetti or other pasta. I also like this with baby spinach leaves instead of rocket and anchovy fillets (first soaked for a few minutes in a little milk) instead of chicken.

chicken and rocket panini

MAKES 2

A little sunflower oil
2 small part-baked baguettes
30 ml/2 tbsp ready-made tomato
    and herb pasta sauce
2 handfuls of wild rocket

4 slices of cooked chicken breast
50 g/2 oz/$^1/_2$ cup grated Mozzarella
    cheese
Freshly ground black pepper

1 Oil the grill and preheat it, then turn it down to the lowest setting.

2 Split the baguettes and open out slightly.

3 Spread the insides with the pasta sauce.

4 Fill with the rocket, chicken and cheese and season with lots of black pepper.

5 Place on the grill. Close the lid and cook for 4 minutes until griddle-browned on both sides and hot through.

You can use a can of creamed mushrooms instead of the cream and fresh mushroom mix – it's equally delicious. If you do use canned mushrooms, add dried mixed herbs instead of oregano for a little more depth of flavour.

creamy mushroom and herb panini

MAKES 2

A little sunflower oil
2 small part-baked baguettes
100 g/4 oz button mushrooms, sliced

30 ml/2 tbsp double (heavy) cream
2.5 ml/½ tsp dried oregano
Salt and freshly ground black pepper

1   Oil the grill and preheat it, then turn it down to the lowest setting.

2   Split the baguettes lengthways, not right through.

3   Mix the mushrooms with the cream, oregano and a little salt and pepper and pack the mixture into the baguettes.

4   Place on the grill, close the lid and cook for 4 minutes until griddle-browned.

This is a great way to use up leftover roast chicken or turkey! You can also try substituting cranberry sauce for the mango chutney and add a pinch of mixed spice instead of the curry paste for a whole new flavour combination.

toasted curried chicken sandwiches

MAKES 2

4 slices of bread
Butter or margarine, for spreading
75 g/3 oz/³/₄ cup chopped cooked
   chicken or turkey

5 cm/2 in piece of cucumber, sliced
15 ml/1 tbsp mango chutney
15 ml/1 tbsp mayonnaise
10 ml/2 tsp mild curry paste

1 Preheat the grill, then turn it down to the lowest setting.

2 Spread the slices of bread on one side with butter or margarine.

3 Mix all the rest of the ingredients together.

4 Put two slices of bread, buttered-sides down, on the grill. Quickly spread the filling over, not quite to the edges.

5 Top with the remaining slices of bread, buttered-sides up. Close the lid and cook for 4 minutes until crisp and griddle-browned.

It sounds grand but this is a simple toasted ham and cheese sarni! I like to add a scraping of English mustard when buttering the top slices of bread for added 'bite'. For best results, go for fairly thick slices of ham.

croque monsieur

MAKES 2

4 slices of bread
Butter or margarine, for spreading
2 thick slices of ham

50 g/2 oz/$^1/_2$ cup grated Cheddar cheese

1 Preheat the grill, then turn it down to the lowest setting.

2 Spread the slices of bread on one side with butter or margarine.

3 Put two slices, buttered-sides down, on the grill. Top with the ham, then the cheese.

4 Top with the other slices of bread, buttered-sides up. Close the lid and cook for 4 minutes until griddle-browned and the cheese has melted.

Corned beef hash is an old-time favourite. Here the mashed meat is flavoured with tomato and spicy Worcestershire sauce before being sandwiched between slices of brown bread and toasted until hot and golden.

hash goldens

MAKES 2

1 x 200 g/7 oz/small can of corned beef
30 ml/2 tbsp tomato ketchup (catsup)

5 ml/1 tsp Worcestershire sauce
4 slices of wholemeal bread
Butter or margarine, for spreading
2 small tomatoes, sliced

1 Preheat the grill, then turn it down to the lowest setting.

2 Mash the corned beef with the tomato ketchup and Worcestershire sauce.

3 Spread the slices of bread with butter or margarine on one side. Put two slices on the grill, buttered-sides down. Spread thickly with the corned beef mixture, then top with the tomatoes.

4 Cover with the other slices of bread, buttered-sides up. Lower the lid and cook for 4 minutes until griddle-browned.

Classic flavour combinations such as cream cheese and smoked salmon can never be beaten. Here they are sandwiched in a bagel, then toasted until the fish is hot and opaque – phenomenal!

toasted cream cheese and smoked salmon bagels

SERVES 2

2 bagels
50 g/2 oz/¼ cup cream cheese
2 slices of smoked salmon

A squeeze of lemon juice
Freshly ground black pepper
Butter or margarine, for spreading

1 Preheat the grill, then turn it down to the lowest setting.

2 Split the bagels. Spread inside with the cheese, then top two halves with the salmon. Sprinkle with lemon juice and add a good grinding of pepper. Cover with the other bagel halves.

3 Spread the tops and bottoms with a little butter or margarine.

4 Place on the grill. Close the lid and cook for 4 minutes.

These sandwiches are gorgeous and taste far more exotic than the simply ingredients would suggest. If you have fresh sage, perhaps from the garden, chop about four leaves for each sandwich; the fragrance and flavour will be really exceptional.

toasted cheese, sage and onion sandwiches

MAKES 2

4 slices of bread
Butter or margarine, for spreading
50 g/2 oz/¹/₂ cup grated Cheddar
   cheese

1 small onion, sliced and separated
   into rings
5 ml/1 tsp dried sage

1 Preheat the grill, then turn it down to the lowest setting.

2 Spread the slices of bread on one side with butter or margarine.

3 Put two slices, buttered-sides down, on the grill. Cover with cheese, then onion rings and a sprinkling of sage.

4 Top with the remaining slices of bread, buttered-sides up. Close the lid and cook for 4 minutes until griddle-browned and the cheese has melted.

These are simply delicious – especially if you don't want anything too rich. However, my family adore them with the addition of a little hot chilli sauce – just pour it on the side of the plate to dip into as you munch.

creamy sweetcorn and celery toasties

MAKES 2

4 slices of bread
Butter or margarine, for spreading
1 celery stick, finely chopped
1 x 200 g/7 oz/small can of
    sweetcorn (corn), drained

30 ml/2 tbsp mayonnaise
30 ml/2 tbsp crème fraîche
2.5 ml/½ tsp dried oregano
Freshly ground black pepper

1 Preheat the grill, then turn it down to the lowest setting.

2 Spread the slices of bread with butter or margarine on one side.

3 Mix the remaining ingredients together.

4 Lay two slices of bread on the grill, buttered-sides down. Spread the corn mixture on top.

5 Top with the remaining bread, buttered-sides up. Close the lid and cook for 4 minutes or until griddle-browned.

A veggie favourite in our household, these are creamy and very tasty. You can use other beans – butter beans are particularly good – and you can also add a little extra crushed garlic or a squeeze of garlic purée if you like more zing.

cheese and borlotti bean batons

MAKES 4

4 baton rolls
1 x 425 g/15 oz/large can of borlotti
  beans, drained
100 g/4 oz/¹/₂ cup soft cheese with
  garlic and herbs
2 sun-dried tomatoes, finely
  chopped

30 ml/2 tbsp chopped fresh basil
Salt and freshly ground black pepper
A little softened butter or margarine,
  for spreading

1 Preheat the grill and turn it down to the lowest setting.

2 Cut a slice off the top of each roll and pull out some of the bread, leaving a 5 mm/¹/₄ in shell.

3 Tip the beans into a bowl and mash well with a fork. Add the remaining ingredients, seasoning the mixture to taste.

4 Spoon the bean mixture into the rolls and top with the 'lids'. Spread butter or margarine sparingly all over the outsides.

5 Place on the grill. If you have an adjustable grill, lower the lid so it rests gently on the batons. If not, lower the lid and support the clip on a cork or similar heat-resistant object, so that the lid just rests on the rolls. Cook for 3 minutes until golden.

You can use salmon instead of tuna if you prefer for these piquant toasted sandwiches and of course you can buy ready-made tartare sauce. I always serve them with a green side salad as they are quite rich.

tuna and tartare sauce toasties

MAKES 2

1 x 185 g/6½ oz/small can of tuna, drained
30 ml/2 tbsp mayonnaise
5 ml/1 tsp pickled capers, chopped
2 cornichons, chopped

15 ml/1 tbsp chopped fresh parsley
Salt and freshly ground black pepper
4 slices of bread
Butter or margarine, for spreading

1   Preheat the grill, then turn it down to the lowest setting.

2   Empty the tuna into a bowl and mash with the mayonnaise. Stir in the capers, cornichons and parsley and season to taste.

3   Spread the slices of bread on one side with butter or margarine.

4   Put two slices, buttered-sides down, on the grill. Top with the tuna mixture, not quite to the edges.

5   Top with the remaining slices of bread, buttered-sides up. Close the lid and cook for about 4 minutes until griddle-browned and hot through.

Sardines are often overlooked but they are cheap and very nutritious. Always mash the bones up with the fish as they are rich in calcium and, as they are so soft, they aren't even noticeable in the finished sandwiches.

piquant sardine and cream cheese bites

MAKES 2

1 x 120 g/4¹/₂ oz/small can of
   sardines in tomato sauce
30 ml/2 tbsp cream cheese
A few drops of Tabasco sauce

Freshly ground black pepper
4 slices of bread
Butter or margarine, for spreading

1 Preheat the grill, then turn it down to the lowest setting.

2 Empty the fish into a bowl and mash thoroughly (including the bones). Mash in the cheese and add a few drops of Tabasco sauce. Season with pepper.

3 Spread one side of the slices of bread with butter or margarine. Place two slices on the grill, buttered-sides down.

4 Top with the sardine mixture, spreading out not quite to the edges.

5 Cover with the remaining slices, buttered-sides up. Close the lid and cook for 4 minutes until griddle-browned.

Hot dog sausages are pretty boring on their own but wrapping them in bacon before griddling gives them a new lease of life. Tucked into soft rolls and smeared with tomato ketchup and Dijon mustard, they make a high-class snack!

griddle dogs

SERVES 4

8 rashers (slices) of streaky bacon, rinded
8 hot dog sausages
15 ml/1 tbsp sunflower oil
8 finger rolls

A few lettuce leaves, torn

TO SERVE:
Tomato ketchup (catsup) and Dijon mustard

1 Preheat the grill.

2 Stretch each rasher of bacon with the back of a knife.

3 Wrap a rasher around each hot dog. Brush with oil.

4 Lay the hot dogs on the grill, close the lid and cook for 4 minutes, turning occasionally, until griddle-browned all over.

5 Split the rolls, not right through, and line with lettuce. Add the hot dogs and some ketchup and mustard. Serve straight away.

These delicious rolls can also be made with pesto – or you could even try a mixture of both. You might find you like an added squeeze of lemon juice on the tapenade to take away the saltiness – try it and see!

tomato and tapenade ciabattas

MAKES 4

A little olive oil
4 ciabatta rolls
60 ml/4 tbsp ready-made tapenade

2 tomatoes, sliced
100 g/4 oz Mozzarella cheese,
   sliced

1 Preheat the grill, then turn it down to the lowest setting.

2 Split the rolls not quite through. Brush the rolls inside and out with olive oil.

3 Spread the tapenade over the insides and then fill with the tomatoes and cheese.

4 Place on the grill. If you have an adjustable grill, lower the lid so it just sits on the rolls. If not, lower the lid and support the clip on a cork or similar heat-resistant object, so that the lid just rests on the rolls. Cook for 4 minutes until griddle-browned.

If you can't get a peach, you can use a chopped satsuma instead – the result will be equally delicious. And if you have a really big appetite, go mad and add two slices of Mortadella to each roll. You can use any salad selection you like.

peach, ricotta and mortadella ciabattas

SERVES 4

1 peach, skinned, halved and stoned (pitted)
30 ml/2 tbsp peach or onion chutney
4 ciabatta rolls
100 g/4 oz/½ cup ricotta or other soft white cheese

4 slices of Mortadella
Freshly ground black pepper
30 ml/2 tbsp olive oil
A few mixed salad leaves, for garnishing

1 Chop the peach finely and mix with the chutney.

2 Preheat the grill, then turn it down to the lowest setting.

3 Cut a slice off the top of each roll and pull out some of the soft bread, leaving a 5 mm/¼ in wall all round.

4 Spread the insides with the cheese, then the peach mixture and top with the Mortadella. Season with a good grinding of black pepper.

5 Brush all over the outsides with olive oil. Place on the grill. If you have an adjustable grill, lower the lid so it just sits on the rolls. If not, lower the lid and support the clip on a cork or similar heat-resistant object, so the lid just rests on the rolls. Cook for 3–4 minutes until griddle-browned.

These flavoursome folded pizzas can be served cold for a packed lunch too. They are best made on an adjustable grill but can be made on one with fixed plates if you prop up the lid, following the instructions in the recipe.

pancetta and mushroom calzones

MAKES 2

1 packet of pizza base mix
A little olive oil
30 ml/2 tbsp tomato purée (paste)
4 slices of pancetta, chopped
6 mushrooms, sliced

6 stoned (pitted) black olives, sliced
50 g/2 oz/½ cup grated Mozzarella cheese
1.5 ml/¼ tsp dried oregano

1 Make up the dough according to the packet directions. Knead gently on a lightly floured surface for five minutes until smooth and elastic.

2 Oil the grill, then preheat it.

3 Cut the dough in half. Roll out each piece to an 18 cm/7 in round. Brush with oil.

4 Turn the dough rounds over and spread the other sides with the tomato purée, not quite to the edges.

5 Pile all the remaining ingredients on one half of each round of dough. Dampen the edges of the dough and fold it over the filling to form semicircles. Press the edges together to seal.

6 Place on the grill. If you have an adjustable grill, lower the lid until it just rests on the dough. If not, lower the lid and support the clip on a cork or similar heat-resistant object, so the lid is just resting on the dough. Cook for 7–8 minutes until griddle-browned and cooked through.

These gorgeous folded pizzas are also delicious made with garlic and herb soft cheese instead of the blue cheese, although you will need to season the filling more thoroughly as Gorgonzola is slightly salty. Dolcelatte works well too.

calzones with spinach and quail's eggs

MAKES 2

1 packet of pizza base mix
A little olive oil
30 ml/2 tbsp tomato purée (paste)
100 g/4 oz frozen chopped spinach, thawed
Salt and freshly ground black pepper

4 quail's eggs
50 g/2 oz/½ cup crumbled Gorgonzola cheese
25 g/1 oz/¼ cup grated Mozzarella cheese
1.5 ml/¼ tsp dried oregano

1 Make up the dough according to the packet directions. Knead gently on a lightly floured surface for five minutes until smooth and elastic. Wrap it in an oiled plastic bag and leave it to rise in a warm place for about 45 minutes.

2 Oil and preheat the grill.

3 Roll out each piece of dough to an 18 cm/7 in round. Brush with oil.

4 Turn the rounds over and spread the other sides with the tomato purée, not quite to the edges.

5 Squeeze the spinach to remove excess water. Spread it over one half of each pizza round. Season lightly. Make two wells in each and break a quail's egg into each well. Top with the cheeses and the oregano.

6 Dampen the edges of the dough, then fold it over the filling and press the edges well together to seal.

7 Place on the grill. If you have an adjustable grill, lower the lid until it just rests on the dough. If not, lower the lid and support the clip on a cork or similar heat-resistant object, so the lid is just resting on the dough. Cook for 7–8 minutes until griddle-browned and cooked through.

The spiciness of the pepperoni and the sweetness of pimiento go so well together in this lovely stuffed pizza. Vary the flavour by adding oregano or basil instead of mixed herbs, or go for chorizo instead of pepperoni.

pepperoni and pimiento calzones

MAKES 2

1 packet of pizza base mix
A little olive oil
30 ml/2 tbsp tomato purée (paste)
50 g/2 oz sliced pepperoni
1 canned pimiento cap, chopped
10 ml/2 tsp capers

50 g/2 oz/½ cup grated Mozzarella cheese
25 g/1 oz/¼ cup grated Cheddar cheese
1.5 ml/¼ tsp dried mixed herbs

1   Make up the dough according to the packet directions. Knead gently on a lightly floured surface for five minutes until smooth and elastic. Wrap it in an oiled plastic bag and leave it to rise in a warm place for about 45 minutes.

2   Oil and preheat the grill, then turn it down to the lowest setting. Knock back (punch down) the dough, then cut it in half. Roll out each piece with a rolling pin to a 20 cm/8 in round. Brush with oil.

3   Turn the rounds over and spread the other sides with the tomato purée, not quite to the edges.

4   Arrange the pepperoni slices on half of each round of dough, not quite to the edges. Top with the pimiento, capers, cheeses and herbs.

5   Dampen the edges and fold the dough over to form semicircles. Press the edges together to seal.

6   Place the calzones on the grill. If you have an adjustable grill, lower the lid until it just rests on the dough. If not, lower the lid and support the clip on a cork or similar heat-resistant object, so the lid is just resting on the dough. Cook for 7–8 minutes until griddle-browned and cooked through.

Seafood pizzas are always popular. You can use ricotta instead of cottage cheese, but it's more expensive! If you don't want to buy artichokes, use a good handful of sliced button mushrooms instead.

artichoke and prawn calzones

SERVES 2

1 packet of pizza base mix
A little olive oil
30 ml/2 tbsp tomato purée (paste)
75 g/3 oz/⅓ cup cottage cheese
   with chives
1 x 425 g/14 oz/large can of artichoke
   hearts, drained and chopped

50 g/2 oz cooked peeled prawns
8 fresh basil leaves, chopped
30 ml/2 tbsp grated Parmesan
   cheese
Freshly ground black pepper

1 Make up the dough according to the packet directions. Knead gently on a lightly floured surface for five minutes until smooth and elastic. Wrap it in an oiled plastic bag and leave it to rise in a warm place for about 45 minutes.

2 Oil and preheat the grill, then turn it down to the lowest setting. Knock back (punch down) the dough, then cut it in half. Roll out each piece with a rolling pin to a 18 cm/7 in round. Brush with oil.

3 Turn over and spread the other sides with the tomato purée, not quite to the edges.

4 Spread the cottage cheese over half of each round. Top with the artichokes and prawns, then scatter the basil over and season with pepper.

5 Dampen the edges and fold the dough over the filling to form semicircles. Press the edges together to seal.

6 Transfer to the grill. If you have an adjustable grill, lower the lid until it just rests on the dough. If not, lower the lid and support the clip on a cork or similar heat-resistant object, so the lid is just resting on the dough. Cook for 7–8 minutes until griddle-browned and cooked through.

SIDE
DISHES

You can use your grill to cook all sorts of vegetables as accompaniments to plain grilled meats, poultry or fish. If you are cooking everything on the grill, I recommend you cook the meat first, then reheat the grill and cook the vegetables immediately before serving. Don't try to keep them warm for very long — they will lose both their food value and texture.

These golden, low-fat slices of potato are so simple to make, taste absolutely wonderful and are not at all greasy. Plus you have the added advantage of avoiding any lingering cooking smells that can hang around after you've been deep-frying.

crispy scalloped potatoes

SERVES 4

Olive oil
2 large potatoes, scrubbed

Coarse sea salt, for garnishing

1   Oil and preheat the grill.

2   Cut the potatoes into 5 mm/¼ in thick slices. Pat dry on kitchen paper (paper towels). Toss in 30 ml/2 tbsp of the olive oil to coat completely.

3   Lay the slices in an even layer on the grill. Close the lid and cook for 25 minutes until crisp and griddle-browned on the outside and soft in the middle.

4   Season with coarse sea salt and serve.

Make as many as you like of these – they are high in fibre and very low in fat. You can use the leftover scooped-out potato for the potato cakes on page 81, as a filling for an omelette (similar to a tortilla) or to thicken soup.

southern-grilled potato skins

SERVES 4

4 large potatoes, scrubbed
30 ml/2 tbsp sunflower oil

FOR THE SEASONING:
5 ml/1 tsp garlic salt

1.5 ml/¼ tsp chilli powder
5 ml/1 tsp mixed (apple-pie) spice
Freshly ground black pepper

1 Prick the potatoes all over with a fork. Bake in the oven at 180°C/350°F/gas mark 4/fan oven 160°C for about 1 hour or until soft. Alternatively, bake in the microwave for about 4 minutes per potato (or according to directions).

2 Cut the potatoes in half and scoop out most of the potato, leaving a wall about 5 mm/¼ in thick. Cut each half into three wedges.

3 Brush all over with oil. Mix the seasoning ingredients together, then sprinkle evenly over the potato skins.

4 Preheat the grill. Lay the skins on the grill, close the lid and cook for about 5 minutes until griddle-striped. Serve hot.

You can use green bananas for this, but they must be really green. If they are already turning yellow, the results will be rather too soft and semi-burnt in the griddle marks instead of crisp and griddle-browned, because of the high sugar content.

plantain chips

SERVES 2–4

2 green plantains
30 ml/2 tbsp sunflower oil

5 ml/1 tsp ground cumin
A little salt

1 Use a sharp pointed knife to cut the skin of the plantains, then peel it off. Cut diagonally into thin slices and place in a bowl.

2 Add the oil and the cumin and toss well so each piece is coated.

3 Preheat the grill. Arrange the plantain slices on the grill. Close the lid and cook for 5 minutes, then turn over and cook for a further 5 minutes or until griddle-striped and fairly crisp.

4 Remove from the grill. Sprinkle with salt before serving.

These are delicious served with omelettes or griddled chicken, or as a side dish with a cauliflower or macaroni cheese for a tasty meal. They also make a great light lunch or supper with some crusty bread and griddled tomatoes.

courgettes with bacon

SERVES 4

4 even-sized courgettes (zucchini)
8 rashers (slices) of streaky bacon

30 ml/2 tbsp sunflower oil
2.5 ml/$\frac{1}{2}$ tsp dried mixed herbs

1 Preheat the grill.

2 Trim the courgettes and cut into halves lengthways.

3 Stretch each rasher of bacon with the back of a knife. Wrap a rasher round each half of courgette. Brush all over with oil and sprinkle with the herbs.

4 Lay the courgettes on the grill, close the lid and cook for about 6 minutes until they are tender and the bacon is griddle-browned.

If you can get corn cobs in their husks, peel back the leaves, smear the unmelted butter and other flavouring ingredients inside, then re-wrap them and griddle them. Peel off the husks at the table. If your cobs are big, cook two at a time.

griddled corn cobs
with sweet spiced orange butter

SERVES 4

4 small corn on the cobs
Finely grated zest and juice of
    1 orange
50 g/2 oz/¼ cup butter

5 ml/1 tsp mixed (apple-pie) spice
Freshly ground black pepper
30 ml/2 tbsp chopped fresh parsley

1 Preheat the grill.

2 Put the orange zest and juice, the butter, spice, a good grinding of pepper and the parsley in a small saucepan. Heat until melted. Brush a little over the corn.

3 Place the corn on the grill. Cook on the open grill for about 15–20 minutes, turning occasionally.

4 Place the corn on warm plates. Pour the melted spiced orange butter over and serve.

These classic Mediterranean flavours combine beautifully for a wonderful accompaniment to any meat, poultry or fish. The addition of the sun-dried tomatoes adds piquancy. You could add a few chopped anchovies as well.

griddled peppers with sun-dried tomatoes and garlic

SERVES 4

15 ml/1 tbsp oil from a jar of sun-dried tomatoes
15 ml/1 tbsp olive oil
4 green (bell) peppers, quartered
4 sun-dried tomatoes in olive oil, finely chopped

2 garlic cloves, finely chopped
Freshly ground black pepper
8 fresh basil leaves, torn, for garnishing

1 Put both the oils in a shallow dish. Add the pepper quarters and toss until they are well coated and glistening.

2 Preheat the grill.

3 Lay the peppers on the grill, cut sides up. Scatter the chopped tomatoes and garlic over each piece and season with pepper.

4 Close the lid and cook for 6–8 minutes.

5 Sprinkle with the basil before serving.

These are slightly crisp on the outside, very sweet and very
moreish. Serve them with everything from steak to sausages.
You could also dip the slices in egg and breadcrumbs before
cooking, but in that case don't separate them into rings.

griddled onion rings

SERVES 4

3 onions, cut into 5 mm/¹/₄ in slices

45 ml/3 tbsp plain (all-purpose) flour

Salt and freshly ground black pepper

30 ml/2 tbsp sunflower oil

1 Preheat the grill.

2 Separate the onions into rings. Mix the flour with a little salt and pepper. Dip the onion rings in the oil and then the flour mixture. Toss until well coated, then shake off excess flour.

3 Place the rings on the grill, close the lid and cook for 5–6 minutes until griddle-striped and cooked through.

4 Serve hot.

This is unusual but very good and very nutritious. The broccoli takes on a toasted appearance in patches on its lovely bright green colour, and the egg sauce adds an interesting twist. You could serve them drizzled with warm passata if you prefer.

grilled broccoli with chopped egg sauce

SERVES 4

1 large head of broccoli,
   cut into 12 florets
30 ml/2 tbsp olive oil

FOR THE SAUCE:
1 hard-boiled (hard-cooked) egg

60 ml/4 tbsp mayonnaise
45 ml/3 tbsp milk
30 ml/2 tbsp chopped fresh parsley
Freshly ground black pepper

1 Preheat the grill.

2 Toss the broccoli in the oil. Place in an even layer on the grill, close the lid and cook for about 5 minutes until brown on top and just tender.

3 Meanwhile, mix the sauce ingredients in a small saucepan and heat through.

4 Transfer the broccoli to small dishes, spoon the sauce over and serve.

Asparagus cooked this way is beautifully green and tender and has a wonderful flavour. When you boil or even steam the spears, some of the flavour is lost in the moisture, but here all the taste and nutrients are retained.

griddled asparagus
with fresh parmesan shavings

SERVES 4

450 g/1 lb thick asparagus spears
60 ml/4 tbsp olive oil
Freshly ground black pepper

50 g/2 oz/¹/₂ cup freshly shaved
Parmesan cheese

1 Preheat the grill.

2 Trim the bases off the stalks of the asparagus. Scrape the stalks if very thick.

3 Brush all over with some of the olive oil. Lay on the grill, close the lid and cook for 3–4 minutes until just tender.

4 Transfer to warm plates, trickle the rest of the olive oil around and scatter with black pepper and Parmesan shavings.

A wonderful mixture of Italian vegetables are combined to make a beautiful dish to accompany any meat, poultry or fish. They are so good, however, you could just sprinkle them with Parmesan and serve them with crusty bread.

mediterranean vegetables with fragrant herbs and garlic

SERVES 4

45 ml/3 tbsp olive oil
1 large garlic clove, crushed
15 ml/1 tbsp chopped fresh
   rosemary
15 ml/1 tbsp chopped fresh basil
1 red (bell) pepper, cut into 8 strips
1 green pepper, cut into 8 strips
1 yellow pepper, cut into 8 strips

1 small aubergine (eggplant), cut
   diagonally into slices
1 large courgette (zucchini), cut
   diagonally into slices
1 red onion, cut into 8 wedges
Coarse sea salt and 30 ml/2 tbsp
   chopped fresh parsley, for
   garnishing

1   Put the oil and garlic in a large bowl and whisk together. Stir in the herbs. Add all the prepared vegetables and toss with your hands to coat completely.

2   Preheat the grill.

3   Lay all the vegetables on the grill. Close the lid and cook for 6–8 minutes until slightly charred in places and tender.

4   Transfer to a warm serving dish, sprinkle with coarse sea salt and chopped parsley and serve hot or cold.

Sprouts always taste good with chestnuts and the addition of feta cheese makes a glorious combination. Don't just reserve them for Christmas, try them with my Sizzling Lamb with Herbs and Garlic (see page 31).

griddled sprouts
with chestnuts and feta cheese

SERVES 4

350 g/12 oz brussels sprouts,
  trimmed
200 g/7 oz cooked peeled chestnuts
15 g/¹/₂ oz/1 tbsp butter

1.5 ml/¹/₄ tsp dried sage
50 g/2 oz/¹/₂ cup crumbled feta
  cheese

1 Blanch the sprouts in boiling water for 2 minutes. Drain and dry thoroughly. Return to the pan.

2 Add the chestnuts, butter and sage and toss until the butter melts.

3 Preheat the grill.

4 Arrange the sprouts and chestnuts on the grill. Close the lid and cook for 3 minutes.

5 Tip into a warm serving dish, add the feta cheese, toss gently and serve straight away.

You will be amazed how much juice comes out of these mushrooms during cooking, so do catch it in the drip tray as it is far too tasty to waste. I recommend you pour it over the finished dish as it is full of flavour.

griddled garlic and thyme mushrooms

SERVES 4

A little sunflower oil
50 g/2 oz/¹/₄ cup butter
1 garlic clove, crushed
30 ml/2 tbsp chopped fresh parsley

15 ml/1 tbsp chopped fresh thyme
Salt and freshly ground black pepper
8 large flat mushrooms, peeled and
  stalks trimmed

1 Oil the grill, then preheat it.

2 Mash the butter with the garlic, half the parsley, all the thyme and a little salt and pepper.

3 Spread the garlic butter over the gills of the mushrooms.

4 Place the mushrooms on the grill, close the lid and cook for 3–4 minutes until tender. Transfer to warm plates and spoon the juices from the drip tray over.

5 Sprinkle with the remaining parsley and serve straight away.

Pretty, tasty, bright green and white vegetable sticks, bathed in a nutty dressing – these make the perfect accompaniment to pork, lamb or chicken. Serve them plain, without the dressing, if your main dish has a rich sauce.

baby leeks with walnut dressing

SERVES 4

16–24 baby leeks
60 ml/4 tbsp olive oil
15 ml/1 tbsp walnut oil
50 g/2 oz/½ cup walnuts, chopped

15 ml/1 tbsp lemon juice
5 ml/1 tsp Dijon mustard
A good pinch of light brown sugar
Salt and freshly ground black pepper

1 Preheat the grill.

2 Trim the leeks and coat in 30 ml/2 tbsp of the olive oil.

3 Lay the leeks on the grill. Close the lid and cook for 5–7 minutes until tender.

4 Meanwhile, whisk the remaining olive oil with all the other ingredients to make a smooth dressing.

5 Transfer the leeks to warm plates and spoon the dressing over.

FRUIT AND SWEET GRILLS

Most people think of grilling only savoury foods but you can use your grill for all kinds of sweet things and desserts too. Here is a selection of really delicious creations to set your taste buds singing. And, best of all, most of them take only a few minutes to prepare and cook.

Bananas and butterscotch are firm favourites. These bananas are griddled until they are nicely browned but still with some texture, then flooded with a sweet, buttery, slightly lemony sauce that tastes just heavenly.

butterscotch bananas

SERVES 4

4 large firm bananas
100 g/4 oz/½ cup butter
175 g/6 oz/¾ cup light brown sugar
45 ml/3 tbsp lemon juice

60 ml/4 tbsp double (heavy) cream

TO SERVE:
Greek-style plain yoghurt

1   Cut the bananas in half lengthways, then in half across the middle.

2   Melt the butter in a small saucepan and brush a little over the bananas.

3   Preheat the grill.

4   Add the sugar and lemon juice to the butter. Heat until the sugar melts, then boil for 1 minute. Stir in the cream.

5   Lay the bananas on the grill and cook for 1–1½ minutes until griddle-browned but still holding their shape.

6   Transfer to warm plates, spoon the butterscotch sauce over and serve with Greek-style plain yoghurt.

You can experiment with other fruits, such as pineapple cubes, plums or even chunks of kiwi fruit, for these simple but lovely kebabs. It's the sweet, buttery bread that makes them so delicious.

crusty strawberry and apricot kebabs

SERVES 4

4 thick slices of French bread, cut
   into quarters
100 g/4 oz/½ cup butter, melted
8 strawberries, hulled

4 apricots, halved and stoned
   (pitted)
Caster (superfine) sugar, for dusting

TO SERVE:
Vanilla ice cream

1   Preheat the grill.

2   Dip the bread cubes in some of the melted butter. Toss the fruit in the remaining butter.

3   Thread the bread alternately with the fruit on wooden skewers that have been soaked in cold water.

4   Lay the kebabs on the grill. Cook on the open grill for about 5 minutes, turning occasionally until lightly griddle-browned.

5   Dust with caster sugar and serve straight away with a scoop or two of ice cream.

This is a very popular flavour combination. The lime brings out the full flavour of the papaya and, when cooked on the griddle, the two taste just wonderful. It's a quick dish to make but looks fabulous so is good enough for any occasion.

grilled papaya with lime

SERVES 2

A little sunflower oil
15 g/½ oz/1 tbsp butter
Finely grated zest and juice of 1 lime
1 small papaya, halved and black
   seeds removed

TO SERVE:
Vanilla ice cream and almond thin
   biscuits (cookies)

1 Oil the grill and preheat it.

2 Mash the butter with the lime zest and juice.

3 Spread the papaya with the lime butter. Place on the grill, close the lid and cook for 2–3 minutes.

4 Transfer to warm plates. Top with a scoop of vanilla ice cream and serve straight away with almond thins.

Cheesecakes are always popular but these are much easier to make than the real thing and perfect for a last-minute end to a meal. Serve them as a dessert, as a teatime treat or even with coffee in the morning. Try them with different sweet breads too.

lemon cheesecake slices

MAKES 4

200 g/7 oz/scant 1 cup Mascarpone
  cheese
Grated zest and juice of 1 lemon
60 ml/4 tbsp caster (superfine)
  sugar, plus extra for dusting

30 ml/2 tbsp sultanas (golden
  raisins)
8 slices of raisin bread
Butter or margarine, for spreading

1 Preheat the grill and turn to the lowest setting. Mix the cheese with the lemon zest, sugar and sultanas. Sharpen with a little of the lemon juice.

2 Spread the slices of bread on one side with butter or margarine. Sandwich together with the cheese mixture, not quite to the edges.

3 Place on the grill, close the lid and cook for 3 minutes until griddle-browned.

4 Sprinkle with a little more sugar before serving.

Fresh pineapple is both sweet and tangy and when it is cooked on a griddle, the flavour bursts into life. The honey nut sauce adds texture and richness and the lemon crème fraîche is just the perfect, cool accompaniment.

fresh pineapple with honey nut drizzle and lemon crème fraîche

SERVES 4

1 pineapple
50 g/2 oz/¼ cup butter
60 ml/4 tbsp clear honey
50 g/2 oz/½ cup toasted chopped
   nuts

Finely grated zest and juice of
   1 small lemon
150 ml/¼ pt/⅔ cup crème fraîche
15 ml/1 tbsp icing (confectioners')
   sugar

1 Cut the top and base off the pineapple. Cut into eight thin slices and cut off all the skin.

2 Preheat the grill.

3 Melt the butter in a small saucepan and brush a little over the slices of pineapple.

4 Mix the honey, nuts and lemon juice into the butter and heat through stirring.

5 Mix the crème fraîche with the lemon zest and icing sugar. Chill until ready to use.

6 Place the pineapple on the grill (do it in two batches if the pineapple is very large). Close the lid and cook for 2 minutes until the sugar is just caramelising on the surface. Transfer to warm plates.

7 Drizzle the honey nut sauce over and serve with the lemon crème fraîche.

This dessert may not be as pretty as some, but it tastes delicious. When you slit the cooked banana, you must take care not to cut through the bottom skin. Then you can ease it open so that the liqueur soaks into the fruit rather than running all over the plate!

quick-cook bananas
with coffee liqueur

SERVES 4

4 bananas
60 ml/4 tbsp coffee liqueur

TO SERVE:
4 scoops of coffee ice cream

1 Oil the grill, then preheat it. Lay the unpeeled bananas on the grill, close the lid and cook for 4–5 minutes until blackened on the outside and soft when squeezed gently.

2 Remove from the grill and place on plates. Split each one along one edge and carefully open. Pour the coffee liqueur into the slit.

3 Serve with a scoop of coffee ice cream on the side.

These are toasted teacakes but with a big difference! They are filled with a rich, sweet vanilla cheese, laced with currants and walnuts, then griddled until warm and slightly crisp on the outside. A lovely dessert or teatime treat.

vanilla and walnut cheesecakes

MAKES 4

200 g/7 oz/scant 1 cup medium-fat soft white cheese
60 ml/4 tbsp icing (confectioners') sugar, plus extra for dusting
25 g/1 oz/¼ cup chopped walnuts

25 g/1 oz/3 tbsp currants
4 ml/¾ tsp vanilla essence (extract)
4 teacakes
25 g/1 oz/2 tbsp softened butter or margarine

1 Preheat the grill, then turn to the lowest setting.

2 Beat the cheese with the sugar, walnuts, currants and vanilla.

3 Cut a thin slice off the top of each teacake and pull out some of the insides, leaving a 5 mm/¼ in wall.

4 Crumble the filling you removed and mix into the cheese mixture. Spoon this mixture into the teacakes and replace the lids.

5 Spread all over the outsides with the butter. If you have an adjustable grill, lower the lid until it just rests on the teacakes. If not, lower the lid and support the clip on a cork or similar heat-resistant object, so the lid is just resting on the teacakes. Cook for 4 minutes until griddle-browned.

6 Dust with a little sifted icing sugar before serving.

Cinnamon is the perfect spice for apples – it brings out the flavour beautifully. This delicious desert is easily put together. You can either make your own pastry or use ready-made shortcrust from the supermarket.

apple and cinnamon turnovers

SERVES 4

2 cooking (tart) apples, peeled, quartered, cored and sliced
15 ml/1 tbsp golden (light corn) syrup
2.5 ml/$^1\!/_2$ tsp ground cinnamon

225 g/8 oz shortcrust pastry (basic pie crust)

TO SERVE:
Custard

1 Put the cooking apples in a saucepan with 15 ml/1 tbsp water. Cover and cook gently for 3 minutes, stirring once or twice, until the apples begin to soften. Stir in the golden syrup and cinnamon and leave to cool.

2 Roll out the pastry and cut into four 18 cm/7 in squares. Spoon the apple mixture into the centres of the squares. Dampen the edges. Take one corner of each pastry square and fold it over diagonally to the opposite point, to form triangles. Press the edges well together, then fold over each edge to seal more thoroughly. Chill until ready to cook.

3 Preheat the grill. Put the turnovers on the grill. If you have an adjustable grill, lower the lid so it just sits on the turnovers. If not, lower the lid and support it on a cork or similar flame-resistant object so the lid just rests on the pastry. Cook for 6 minutes until griddle-browned and cooked through.

4 Serve with custard (and more warmed syrup if you have a sweet tooth).

These little chocolate croissants cook beautifully on the grill, and they marry perfectly with pear quarters, grilled until golden and caramelised with just a sprinkling of sugar. They are best served straight away – you won't be able to resist them anyway!

griddled chocolatines
with caramelised pear quarters

SERVES 4

A little sunflower oil
2 pears, cut into quarters
25 g/1 oz/2 tbsp butter, melted
20 ml/4 tsp light brown sugar

4 mini chocolatines
Bottled chocolate sauce for ice
   cream

1   Oil the grill and preheat it. Brush the pears with a little of the butter and sprinkle with the sugar.

2   Place on the grill, close the lid but don't clip it together. Cook for 30 seconds, then clip it shut and cook for 1½ minutes. Remove from the grill and keep warm.

3   Brush the chocolatines with the remaining butter. Lay them on the grill and cook on the open grill for 1–2 minutes on each side, pressing down lightly with a spatula, until crisp.

4   Place the chocolatines on warm plates with two pear quarters on each. Drizzle the fruit with a little chocolate sauce and serve straight away.

These are best cooked on an adjustable grill. If you use a fixed-plate one, support the lid with a cork or similar heat-resistant object. If you close the lid, the end product will be flat and the filling might ooze, although it will still taste good.

banana, chocolate and coconut turnovers

SERVES 4

1 banana
30 ml/2 tbsp plain (semi-sweet)
  chocolate spread
15 ml/1 tbsp desiccated (shredded)
  coconut
225 g/8 oz shortcrust pastry (basic
  pie crust)

15 ml/1 tbsp icing (confectioners')
  sugar, for dusting

TO SERVE:
Cream

1   Mash the banana, chocolate spread and coconut together.

2   Roll out the pastry and cut into four 18 cm/7 in squares. Spoon the banana mixture into the centres of the squares. Dampen the edges. Take one corner of each pastry square and fold it over diagonally to the opposite point, to form triangles. Press the edges well together, then fold them over to seal more completely. Chill until ready to cook.

3   Preheat the grill.

4   Put the turnovers on the grill. If you have an adjustable grill, lower the lid so it just sits on the turnovers. If not, lower the lid and support it on a cork or similar heat-resistant object so that the lid just rests on the pastry (paste). Cook for 6 minutes until griddle-browned and cooked through.

5   Dust with sifted icing sugar and serve warm with cream.

These little inverted trifles taste absolutely delicious – especially with a dollop of clotted or whipped cream on the side. For added effect, you could grate some chocolate or crumble a Flake bar round the edges of the plates before serving.

black forest bites

MAKES 4

4 trifle sponges, split into halves
Butter or margarine, for spreading
30 ml/2 tbsp plain (semi-sweet)
　　chocolate spread
30 ml/2 tbsp black cherry jam
　　(conserve)

15 ml/1 tbsp icing (confectioners')
　　sugar

TO SERVE:
Clotted or whipped cream

1   Preheat the grill and turn to the lowest setting.

2   Spread the sponges on the uncut sides with butter or margarine. Spread two with chocolate spread, then jam, on the cut sides. Top with the other sponge halves, buttered-sides out.

3   Place on the grill. Cook on the open grill for 2 minutes, pressing down lightly with a spatula. Turn over and cook for $1\frac{1}{2}$–2 minutes until griddle-browned and the chocolate is just melting.

4   Transfer to small plates and dust with the sifted icing sugar.

5   Serve with clotted or whipped cream.

A touch of nostalgia here – hot crumpets for tea – but, instead of toasting them on the open fire, you can cook them, ready-buttered and sweetened, on your grill. Too much syrup may not be good for you, but everyone deserves a treat now and again!

syrup-soaked crumpets

SERVES 4

20 g/³/₄ oz/1¹/₂ tbsp butter, softened
30 ml/2 tbsp golden (light corn) syrup
4 crumpets

60 ml/4 tbsp thick Greek-style plain
yoghurt (optional)

1 Preheat the grill.

2 Beat the butter with the syrup and spread over the crumpets.

3 Place on the grill. If you have an adjustable grill, lower the lid so that it rests gently on top of the crumpets and cook for 2–3 minutes. If not, cook on the open grill for 2 minutes, then turn the crumpets over and cook for a further 2 minutes, pressing down lightly with a spatula.

4 Transfer to plates and serve topped with spoonfuls of plain Greek-style yoghurt, if liked.

A simple dessert for when you don't know what else to serve, this is easily put together from storecupboard ingredients. It is important to use a crisp green apple – the red ones are too soft and don't have enough flavour for cooking.

griddled apple slices
with lemon and syrup sauce

SERVES 4

3 Granny Smith apples
20 g/³/₄ oz/1¹/₂ tbsp butter, softened
90 ml/6 tbsp golden (light corn)
   syrup

30 ml/2 tbsp lemon juice

TO SERVE:
Cream, custard or plain yoghurt

1   Preheat the grill.

2   Cut the tops and bases off the apples and cut each fruit into four thick slices. Remove the cores.

3   Smear on both sides with the butter.

4   Place on the grill, close the lid and cook for 3 minutes.

5   Meanwhile, heat the syrup and lemon juice in a saucepan until hot but not boiling, stirring all the time.

6   Transfer the apple slices to warm plates and pour the syrup sauce over.

7   Serve with cream, custard or plain yoghurt.

INDEX